BODY
PARTS

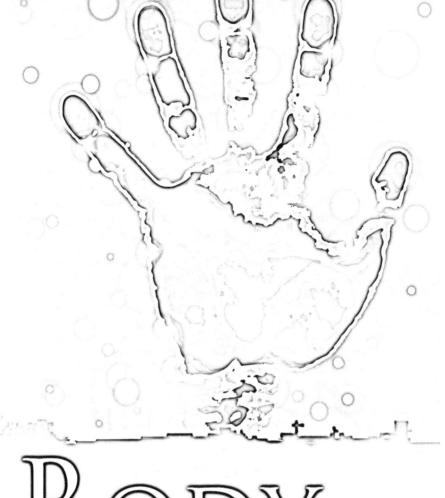

BODY PARTS

FRANK HANKS

Body Parts
by Frank Hanks

Copyright © 2013 by Frank Hanks

All Scripture quotations are taken from the King James Version of the Holy Bible, which is in the public domain.

PUBLISHER CONTACT INFO

E-mail
emptyhospitals@gmail.com

Website
www.emptyhospitals.org

Mailing Address
Empty Hospitals Publishing
PO Box 28013 Highland Green
Red Deer, AB. T4N 7C2
Canada

Empty Hospitals Publishing
The miracle of ink and paper

DEDICATION

I dedicate this book to the Great Holy Spirit of God. He has been my teacher and mentor in all things pertaining to the Kingdom of God. Our walk together is never boring because he is showing me things to come and showing me how to walk in his power. His anointing is the tether by which I abide in the vine.

He has taught me that I need not wait on Him, but that all I need do is take action moved by the needs I see around me, speaking the word of the Lord which activates the unction directing me in the moment bringing the very power of God, unleashing miracles, signs and wonders.

The seven pillars he has hewn out within me created an environment of sustainable breakthrough. Explosive power and unrivaled authority are resident within and accessible at will. The same authority that Jesus has and all the rewards won through His faithfulness are ours to explore and utilize for Kingdom purposes.

It is the Great Holy Ghost that has been given the mandate to mentor the king within as we undergo the predestinated purpose of God; conforming to the very image of Jesus Christ. It is the Great Holy Ghost that is breathing on us again, stirring us to dream bigger than we ever have before. We are going to be part of a staggering paradigm shift historically unprecedented within the Body of Christ. The great Holy Ghost is just getting warmed up.

Thank you, Holy Spirit.

Contents

INTRODUCTION

I n 1989, I attended a conference put on by businessman and Bible teacher Dr. Norvel Hayes. During one of his sessions, he spoke of many instances where God had placed a brand new heart in the chest of someone who needed one. I was amazed by Dr. Hayes' many stories of those who had received this miracle.

During another session, he spoke of a woman who had a strong desire for children but because she had had uterine cancer, her womb had been surgically removed. As she sat listening to Dr. Hayes, God saw her desire and performed a miracle. By the end of the session, she had a brand new womb. Dr. Hayes recounted that during his entire session, nobody touched the woman or prayed for her; instead, she received a new womb by a single sovereign act of the Almighty God. From Dr. Hayes' account, he believed that God rewarded her for sitting through the entire meeting, which lasted six hours.

For me, the importance was not where her womb came from or how it got into her body, but in the realization that God had so connected with this woman, that even a missing womb could not stop Him from fulfilling her desire to have children.

I am so grateful to know such a God.
When a person desires to make an authentic connection
with Him, a spiritual transaction takes place that leaves
little doubt of His power and His love.

I am in awe by how much God loves us and what lengths He goes to redeem us. He sent His son Jesus from Heaven to demonstrate the faith of God for us and to command us to do the same works that Jesus did and greater.

I listened to Dr. Hayes with a child-like curiosity and wondered two things: whether anyone could *believe* for these miracles and whether a person had to be more special than another to *do* the works of God.

Dr. Hayes said that God can only use a person if he or she has acquired the knowledge of God's will in a specific area. In other words, if a person was never taught to cast out devils, that person will probably not be used of God to do so. If a person doesn't understand that God uses people to heal others, then that same person probably won't heal too many people; and, if healing does occur, that person won't understand why or how it happened.

The revelation I acquired from Dr. Hayes is this:

> *God can do anything*
> *and all things are possible*
> *to the person who believes.*

Although Dr. Hayes was misunderstood and criticized for some of the things he said about faith, people under his ministry were healed, and that is what counts when people need a miracle.

The questions began to take shape in my mind: "Could I perform miracles? Could I heal the sick? Could I raise the dead?" Thank God the answer was yes. I could do whatever God said I could do *if I believed*. I decided then that I wanted to *do* the works of God.

> Verily, verily, I say unto you, He that believeth on me, the works that I do shall he do also; and greater works than these shall he do; because I go unto my Father. (John 14:12)

Jesus said it, and so I began my journey to understand how and why I could do what He does.

Praise the Lord
for giving me the Holy Spirit
who would show me how.

At the start of my journey, I was hopeful to be used of God in the kind of power that dramatically alters a persons' life for the better, but I was not sure if I would be an acceptable candidate. However, one thing was clear—I needed knowledge. And so I began Dr. Hayes' two-year Bible study course and learned how to do the works of Jesus. At the time I was attending, the school was not accredited and did not offer a degree. But I believe my education was better than any degree I could have studied for because I got to know God. I got to know (to some degree) how He thinks and to realize that His love for us compels Him to action.

If I am compelled to action by the love of God,
then God's power in me is my result.

You may be wondering if miracles are reserved for the special ones or whether you can participate as well. My experience has shown me that anyone born again can perform miracles and can be empowered to do so. Through education, which includes hands on experience, the gifts of the Holy Spirit, and knowing that Jesus qualifies anyone by simply believing on Him, you too can perform miracles.

The purpose of this book is to

1. Bring awareness of unusual miracles that God can perform through anyone. These miracles can be as unusual as the provision of new body parts to replace defective or missing ones.

2. Create a desire in you to become active in ministering to others. By being active in ministry, you have the potential to awaken multitudes to realize that each one of us can do the works of God.

3. Expose the blockages to wholeness that results from not discerning the Lord's body through communion. Once exposed, this knowledge reverses the effect that these blockages have on sickness, weakness and premature death.

4. Show how these revelations are part of God's plan in training and deploying a mature army of miracle workers—miracle workers who will cause the knowledge of the glory of God to spread like wildfire worldwide.

5. See multitudes glorifying God as they see your good works.

1

Heaven's Storehouses

S pare body parts do exist. In Heaven, there is no lack of anything required to perform His word. If you are willing to serve Him, what you need is in abundant supply. You have access to the storehouses in the Kingdom of Heaven and can appropriate freely exactly what is required, at any given time.

There are body parts in the Kingdom of God for anyone who accesses them by faith. May you become hungry to work with God in His kingdom. *If this seems abnormal to you, it's because your mind has not yet been transformed to agree with Heaven.* The Kingdom of Heaven is here on Earth right now. Miracles can happen right now. You can heal the sick, in this very moment! That's the Kingdom of Heaven. God is glorified every time a believer in Christ performs a miracle. He is pleased when we imitate him. He wants to bring us into a competency and then release us with even more of his glory. Our birthright is to walk with a full complement of Heaven's empowerments and assistance.

> And great multitudes came unto him, having
> with them those that were lame, blind, dumb,

> maimed, and many others, and cast them down
> at Jesus' feet; and he healed them; insomuch
> that the multitude wondered, when they saw
> the dumb to speak, the maimed to be whole,
> the lame to walk, and the blind to see: and they
> glorified the God of Israel. (Matthew 15:30–31)

This Scripture states that Jesus healed people with various illnesses. Some were missing limbs, some were mute, some were crippled, some were lame, and some were blind, and He healed them all. Multitudes were in wonder when they saw the mute begin to speak, the crippled become whole, the lame walk and the blind see, and they glorified the God of Israel.

What Jesus did in this Scripture, you can do also and greater. This means that to the new creation, He has removed all limits or limitations. You can do all of these works of Jesus and more—I prophecy that you will—you will rise to the occasion.

I prophecy that great grace be upon you as you obey the command of Jesus to do the works He did and greater; great grace is found in the prophetic declaration of the power of His resurrection. Declare the kingdom and you will release the power of the resurrection that will cause the miracle. You too will see it with your own eyes!

You can declare the kingdom by beginning to say to yourself these two statements:

1. Miracles are easy for me because I believe in Christ.

2. What He said I can do, I can do; I believe Jesus.

Talk yourself out of any belief that runs contrary to what Jesus says about you. Repeat what He says in Scripture out loud to yourself, until your heart agrees and you are quick to refuse any words or ideas that would try to exalt themselves against the knowledge of God.

> **" Imagination is more important than knowledge.**
>
> **~ Albert Einstein**

Take captive every thought that disagrees with Jesus. Repent of your unbelief and believe the Gospel. Decide for yourself that you will tap into the supply of the spirit of Jesus Christ and bring new body parts to those in need.

Once during a time of prayer, I imagined a room in Heaven full of internal organs: hearts, kidneys, livers, and an assortment of other body parts. I began to grab them and stuff them into my belly for several minutes. I decided that if they are needed by people I encounter daily, then I would be wise to claim as many of them as I can and bring them back to Earth to impart to others. I reasoned that if I stored them in my belly, I would be able to push them out by the rivers of living water that flow out of my belly.

My imagination is a very useful tool for seeking first the Kingdom of God and His righteousness. I like to imagine myself in ministry settings working miracles in an atmosphere void of any unbelief. I imagine complete success each and every time. Unbelief is not allowed in this secret domain of my imagination. I see myself growing out new limbs, healing the sick, casting out devils, and raising the dead. There is no such thing as failure in Heaven. So I convince myself through these exercises that there is no failure where I am at. After practicing in my imagination many times, I can create the same atmosphere when I am in real ministry situations. I try to imagine miracles that are extraordinary. I don't know if I do this to keep God interested, or to keep myself stretching to believe the impossible.

A man of God, Pastor John Onekele, who leads a congregation of more than 1,200 people in Nigeria, who has raised three people from the dead, and who operates in signs and wonders, needed a miracle.

He had swelling in his leg which became very painful. He went to see a doctor who ran some tests, which concluded that Pastor John had a problem with his heart.

During a telephone conversation, I was asked to pray for Pastor John. I told Pastor John that I would not pray for him to be healed, but I would command that a new heart be put into his chest in the name of Jesus. He agreed to that and I did exactly what I said I would do.

I asked him if he felt anything in his chest. He said he did feel something and that he believed he received a brand-new heart. Because Pastor John was in the hospital at the time of our prayer, confirmation of the miracle was done quickly, and he left the hospital in short order. I was told the doctor looking after Pastor John expressed he had never witnessed anything like that miracle.

That was my second experience where someone had received a new heart over the telephone. There have been many who received as I laid hands on them and prayed. As well, two people received new hearts during a trip to Africa in 2011. This is a common miracle for me. I was fortunate that the Lord Jesus exposed me very early in my walk to others who imagined and believed that unusual miracles were possible. When you imagine and believe for such manifestations, they happen; it is that simple. Although it was not always simple for me, it is now. Now I can believe God for unusual miracles.

When I first began performing miracles, my prayers were based more in hope than in knowing. I had more hope than faith, but the hope in God that has come from experiencing the reality of His power has caused me to change. Now I am able to take Him at His word and know by experience that His power is available to do these things. Now I pray with certainty of result. My prayer has become a prayer of faith. My truth is that experience produces hope, and hope ensures that I will not be ashamed. In this area of prayer, I have overcome most of the unbelief that limits miracles. Part of my journey was to come to the place in my believing on Christ, where I could believe that I could also do the works He said I could.

I began to realize that not only hearts, but other needed organs and body parts were as easily accessible and available. You, too, can keep adding to your spiritual tool bag with the intent of becoming even more useful to the body of Christ.

I impart gifts of healings to brand-new believers, then put them right to work healing the sick. I instruct them, showing them exactly what to do and walk them through a few successful healings. They are able to do exactly what I have told them they could do. I try to work with believers who receive an impartation right away.

An example of this was in Nigeria in 2010, where I ministered in a setting where 25 widows had gathered. Before the meeting, the ministry gave us a file for each widow, which stated some personal facts such as the number of children they had. Each of the widows had also written about what they wanted in life. Many of them wrote they wanted business opportunities or education for their children. Widows who live in a country where there are no social services face tough financial challenges. They must pay out-of-pocket for their child's schooling and medical treatment. If they do not have the financial resources, their children do not receive an education or many die from treatable illnesses.

The ministry team I was a part of spoke with them briefly. We told them we would call them up one at a time for prayer, and we told them to think about what they wanted to ask God for and that we would pray that God would grant their request. We also said that we would ask God what He wanted to do for each of them and that we would tell them.

We called up a young widow named Angelina. We prayed for her according to her desires, and then we heard from God. He was calling her to be a leader in her community, especially among the other widows, and he wanted to impart to her gifts of healings and working of miracles. Rather than return her to her seat, we asked her to stay with us and help us pray for the other widows. She was delighted. Person after person came up with some type of sickness or disease.

We taught Angelina how to use authority to command diseases to leave their bodies. She laid hands on all who came to her for prayer and they were healed instantly; praise God! Jesus was true to His word. Angelina left that day, established in her ministry of bringing healing to others, having had lots of opportunity to help deliver others from sickness right in her own community. She will never forget how.

In the same way that a father takes his son by the hand and shows him how to do something, I take new believers by the hand and insist that God will empower them to do miracles. The results are amazing. Any parent knows that speaking encouraging words to a child empowers the child to try. When they try, they discover that they can do what you told them they could. The joy that a parent feels for their child's success is similar to the joy you can feel when you share in a new believer's excitement of accomplishment.

This is an example of how the elder Christian can teach the young Christian, prophetically insisting that they will do the works of Christ. A prophetic word and purposefully finding people who are sick to practice on, establishes the young believer in doing the works of Christ. Just as a child is excited by a new accomplishment, a young believer may become so excited that they sneak around behind your back and start healing people all by themselves.

By repeating what Jesus testifies about doing His works, I am releasing the faith of Christ. The testimony of Jesus Christ is the spirit of prophecy.

> And I fell at his feet to worship him. And he said
> to me, See thou do it not: I am thy fellow-ser-
> vant, and of thy brethren that have the testi-
> mony of Jesus: worship God: for the testimony
> of Jesus is the spirit of prophecy. (Revelation
> 19:10)

Speaking His testimony prophetically opens a supernatural door and invites the anointing of God to carry out that which has been prophesied. Every miracle, sign or wonder gives witness to the resurrection of Jesus Christ. If He was not raised from the dead, there would be no miracles.

> And with great power gave the apostles witness
> of the resurrection of the Lord Jesus: and great
> grace was upon them all. (Acts 4:33)

Many wish to become adept at soul winning. Bringing the power of God in signs and wonders gets the attention of people around you. Entire families can come to Christ because of a single miracle. Groups of people will come to God because they see that He is in you.

When I first saw others perform the miracles that Jesus did in Matthew 15:30–31, I was in awe. Up to that moment, I never knew anyone who could do what Jesus had done. My real shock came when He told me that He expected me to do the very works that He did. He doesn't lie, so I knew I needed to believe Him and begin preparing myself. I began to see some progress, especially with baptizing people in the Holy Spirit and leading others to Christ. After one year in Bible College, I began to see impossible miracles take place.

Have you ever wondered why we do more talking about illness and infirmities than we do praying for those who need healing? I am not talking about praying remotely for people, but about laying hands on them. It occurred to me that if I were to spend more time laying hands on people, then I would see more miracles. I began to look for opportunities to get my hands on people.

One day while at the soup kitchen, I was asked to prepare a short message to preach before we fed the people. My turn came and I remember preaching on some of the encounters people had in the Bible when they encountered Jesus in His Glory. Their natural response was to fall on their faces like dead men. They were encountering God, and although His glory was awe inspiring, it was even more fear provoking. He always told them not to fear. I suggested to my audience in the soup kitchen that if they met me, they might not be affected; but if they came to *encounter Jesus, then everything could change instantly.*

After I finished preaching, a man who was lame from a stroke he suffered came forward. His wife lay dying in the hospital, and he asked if I would be willing to say a prayer for her. I told him that after we ate, I would pray for his wife.

I cannot recall the man's name, but he sat and talked with me as we ate. A stroke victim will usually have one side or the other affected by the stroke. In his case, both his right arm and leg were stiff and barely movable. His face drooped a bit on the right side and his speech was not clear.

He shared with me that he had spent most of his adult life in prison. I asked him what he did time for. He explained that his first time in prison was for murder. A man said something he didn't like, so he blew his brains out. This statement took my breath away. He said it quite matter-of-factly, as if that was the appropriate response. He continued explaining that the second time was for murder also; he had shot and killed another man.

Then he talked about his stroke and how he could no longer use his arm because it had seized up. He shared that he has had thoughts about taking a shotgun and blowing his arm off. I pleaded with him not to do such a drastic thing and he reasoned that his arm was just in the way. I could not imagine the hopelessness he was feeling and the fear he held of losing his wife.

I asked him to stand so we could pray for his wife. I laid hands on him and began saying a prayer for his wife that lasted three or four minutes. Then I began to pray for him. As I prayed, anger rose up in me; I began taking authority over Satan and commanded him to release this man's body and commanded his body to respond to the word of God. I quoted Scriptures about healing and kept ordering his body to respond. Before I knew what was happening, his right arm began to move, his hand began to work again, and a look of amazement came over his face. He smiled and started shouting "praise God" while running around the soup kitchen rejoicing. He ran continuously for a few minutes celebrating what Jesus had done for him. The place was electric as he glorified God like I had never seen before. This miracle caused him to receive Jesus as his Savior and to become very excited about his fresh start with God. About a year later, I called and inquired about that man. I was told that he and his wife were on fire for God, and his whole life was changed when he encountered the power of God in that soup kitchen.

I believe I was more shocked than he was at the events that occurred in that soup kitchen that day. I could not reconcile in my mind with what had just happened. I was spiritually shell-shocked. I had witnessed a man made whole in a second of time. It was the first time I had been a part of such a mind-blowing miracle. Not my first miracle, but my first one so visually stunning.

One thing that was settled for me for all time was that I could do the works of Christ. It was not a fluke. Evidence ends all arguments. When you have done something impossible, it changes you. I know my Father in Heaven was rejoicing as He watched one of His sons perform a miracle. How proud He must be when faith is tested in one of His children, and it passes the test.

In Nigeria in 2011, I had the opportunity to minister to Muslims while going house to house. I had never prayed for Muslims before this, so I was doing the best I could, but I was struggling in a way that may happen when you are unsure of yourself while experiencing something for the first time.

That evening when I was talking to the Lord about my experience, I asked, "What do I do Lord?" He said, "You have more in common with them than you think; Abraham is your common ground." I thought about this for a while. Abraham is relevant to Jews, Christians, and Muslims. They believe in Abraham, so that is where God wanted me to start. So I began to talk to Muslims about Abraham being a friend of God. I shared how God made a covenant with Abraham, saying that He would bless him and that his descendants would be more in number than the stars in the sky. I shared how God said that every family on Earth would be blessed because of this covenant. I then told them that as a Christian, I had discovered the secret of getting the blessing of Abraham for myself. The blessing was to come by faith in Jesus Christ. I told them that Jesus brought the blessing of Abraham to us.

Every family we spoke with had at least one to three people currently suffering from illnesses such as malaria, tuberculosis, and typhoid. I told them that I would ask that God keep His covenant with Abraham and bless them. I told them that I would ask him to do so in the name of Jesus. I told them that if I were right, they would receive healing instantly when I laid my hands on them to pray. No one turned down my offer to pray. Every single person that day and everyone on that trip was instantly healed of whatever was wrong with them.

God backed up His word. They were all healed. Understanding how serious God was when He made this promise to Abraham was the doorway in setting many Muslims free. *It was also a tremendous revelation to me that the covenant between God and Abraham was serious enough to God to still endure today in Christ Jesus for the asking.* I sometimes wonder how we can have such a wonderful God who has made such sure promises, and yet we do not enter into them.

When God made these promises to Abraham, do you think He might have known that the sons and daughters of Abraham might not be blessed without a new arm, leg, kidney, liver, heart, thyroid gland or countless other needs that would be required to make them whole? I believe that He knew that; I believe that He made provision for these things, and I believe that as His servants, we should neglect no one in telling them that Jesus is a healer.

I have been ashamed on several occasions where I've seen someone who needed a miracle for healing, but because of my unbelief, I shied away from preaching the gospel of healing. The shame intensified afterwards, when I realized I had been a coward to not love them enough to push past my doubts and truly believe for them.

I cannot say I have the full picture. But, if I am successful to introduce you to Jesus as He really is, you, too, will see that we are at the beginning of a great awakening that will unlock the resources of Heaven to you and many others who have seen the blessing of Abraham firsthand.

May we see Jesus so clearly that we fall on our face as dead men, forever changed from the experience, knowing that we are able to do what He has called us to do.

May God empower you and reveal Himself to you. May everything He has placed in His kingdom within you, become fruitful. No more bareness in the Body of our Lord. May He use you to bring the body parts. No limitations God! Take us into the holiest place.

2

LIMITATIONS REMOVED
IN CHRIST

There are several limiting beliefs imposed on the Body of Christ by misinformed teachers and ministers. While well-meaning, these limiting beliefs become part of the filter that is used to understand the Kingdom of God. When the lens is distorted due to false or limiting beliefs, kingdom results are impeded. This cannot work. Christ cautioned against the leaven of the Pharisees and of Herod, who manipulated the law and the people's perception of it until there remained no freedom, only more rules and enslavement. His warning was not only for His day, but remains critically important in every generation. It is this leaven that causes the Body to become powerless and on the defensive, when we are meant to be powerful and aggressive.

This chapter will help you understand two blockages or limiting beliefs that prevent us from ruling with Christ in this life. Once we understand the lies that have limited the Kingdom of God within us, we then have a choice to repent and believe the gospel.

When we believe lies, we are walking in the dark, unable to take the limiting beliefs off. But when the light comes, the darkness is exposed, freeing us from the blinders that have kept us from walking in the glory of the resurrected Christ. There are two lies that spread unbelief:

LIE 1: ONLY GOD HEALS

Although this statement seems accurate, it is one made in ignorance. The message communicates the intent of putting our whole trust in what God can do. Although the intent seems necessary, the limitation this statement implies is that we are separate from God instead of being one with him. Although healing did originate in Him, *He has also delegated that same healing to His Body on Earth*, namely all of those who have followed Christ into the regeneration, being born of Spirit and of water into the Family of God. Now are we the sons of God through birth, by the Last Adam—Jesus Christ. (See John 3:5–6, Titus 3:5, and 1 John 3:2)

When I make the statement that I've healed someone, often the response is, "Only God can heal," or "God did the healing, not you."

The argument against these responses is that if I am the body of Christ and I am healing others using His Name and through faith in His name, am I claiming glory apart from Christ? No, because it is by *His* power that I am doing His works, but I am the one who is healing in His name; He already did His part as is evidenced by the stripes on His back. The work being done now is the work completed by His body on Earth, under the authority delegated to His body. His body is doing the works, but works are limited to those within the body who *believe*. Those who believe succeed in His work because they understand their authority to do the work; obeying the Lord by completion of the work.

> But God, who is rich in mercy, for his great love
> wherewith he loved us, even when we were dead
> in sins, hath quickened us together with Christ,
> (by grace ye are saved), and hath raised us up
> together, and made us sit together in heavenly
> places in Christ Jesus. (Ephesians 2:4–6)

This Scripture shows a crucial juncture in the understanding of a saint.

A spiritual identity crisis infects the body: separation from God. If you incorrectly discern the Lord's body, you do not understand who you are in Christ. The truth is that you are seated with Christ. You are raised up with Him. You have been called to rule with Him in *this* life. Does ruling with Him mean that you are ruling over sickness and diseases? Yes. Does ruling with Him mean that you are ruling with Him over death? Yes. Does ruling with Him mean that you are ruling against the works of the enemy? Yes.

When we do not discern the Lord's body and we do not take our place with Him, we reject our positional authority.

Why pray that God will do something that He cannot do without you? I am rejecting the positional authority He gave me when I think I am not qualified to do what He has called me to do. However, when I take ownership of my positional authority with Christ, I step into the position of King. A king uses all the authority he has to rule. Jesus has been given all authority in Heaven and in Earth. Does that mean He asks us to grab a comfortable chair and watch Him work? No. After He said He had been given this authority, He turned to *us* and said *go*.

> And Jesus came, and spoke to them, saying, all
> power is given to me in Heaven and upon Earth.
> Go ye therefore and teach all nations, baptiz-
> ing them in the name of the Father, and of the
> Son, and of the Holy Spirit. Teaching them to

> observe all things whatever I have commanded
> you: and lo, I am with you always, even to the
> end of the world. Amen. (Matthew 28:18–20)

When you rule with someone, you share their authority. Authority is recognized in the spiritual realm. It is recognized by all of our enemies. When we take our authority, our enemies lose. It's that simple. They lose and we win. We overcome our enemies by the blood of the Lamb and by the word of our testimony. If the word of our testimony is that we rule and reign with Christ, we heal the sick, cast out devils and are positioned in Christ with all power in Heaven *and* in Earth. We put our enemies to flight.

Consider a scenario where 20 people pray that God will heal a sick person and nothing happens. Then the twenty-first person begins to pray and commands the sickness to leave the sick person's body, and suddenly the person is set free. Can you explain what happened?

Ask yourself these questions.

- Did I become one with Him in His death?
- Did I become one with Him in His burial?
- Did I become one with Him in His resurrection?
- Was I raised with Him and made to sit with Him in heavenly places?

You may be answering yes to all these questions, but when it comes to doing the works He said that we would do, confusion creates a great gulf between what He commanded us to do and what we are actually doing in His name. Unfortunately, we wrongly discern that we should be very careful not to say anything that draws any attention to ourselves. But Jesus taught differently.

> Let your light so shine before men, that they
> may *see your good works*, and glorify your Father

which is in Heaven. Think not that I am come
to destroy the law, or the prophets: I am not
come to destroy, but to fulfill. (Matthew 5:16–
17, italics mine)

Consider carefully the words of the apostles Peter and John.

Then Peter said: Silver and gold have I none;
but such as *I have give I thee*. In the name of Jesus
Christ of Nazareth, rise up and walk. (Acts 3:6,
italics mine)

Peter was clear in declaring that *he* possessed something
he could give. Peter gave to the man something *he* had been
given. Peter took ownership of what *he had*. He was stewarding
something that God *had given him*.

And as ye go, preach, saying, the Kingdom of Heaven is at hand. Heal the sick,
cleanse the lepers, raise the dead, cast out
devils: freely *ye have received, freely give.*
(Matthew 10:7–8, italics mine)

Did Jesus tell them that *He would go with them and heal
people for them*? No; instead, He sent them out *fully expecting
them to heal the sick.*

*You may want to say yes,
but perhaps religion has threatened you;
caused you to shy away from making your claim
to what Jesus has given you.*

What did God give to Peter? What commodity resided in
Peter? Obviously, it carried the authority of God and the ability
to materialize. Obviously, the anointing to do a miracle was
contained in what Peter had received. Have you received what

Peter possessed? If so, have you acknowledged it? If so, do you use this power?

Do you accept it when religion devalues and denies what you have received from Christ? I hope you say no; the body of Christ *needs you* to become functional and proficient in putting to work that which has been invested in you for kingdom purposes. *You are no different than Peter. You too have been given a supply of the Spirit of Jesus Christ and all the weighty power of Heaven and Earth vested in that name.*

> And whatsoever ye shall ask in my name, that will I do, that the Father may be glorified in the Son. If ye shall ask any thing in my name, I will do it. (John 14:13–14)

The word *ask* in the above verse correctly translated is *command.*

> Whatsoever you *command* to be done, using my name, I will agree to it, that the father may be glorified in the Son.

Peter and John had been given His *name.* His *name* releases the kingdom within you to heal those around you by faith in Christ.

> And *His name through faith in His name hath made this man strong,* whom ye see and know: yea, the faith which is by him hath given him this perfect soundness in the presence of you all. (Acts 3:16, italics mine)

The faith they were activating was the faith that had been given to them of Christ.

> And as ye go, preach, saying: The Kingdom of Heaven is at hand. Heal the sick, cleanse the lepers, raise the dead and cast out

devils: freely *ye have received, freely give.*
(Matthew 10:7–8, italics mine)

Luke 10:17–20 explains what happened when Peter and John returned from their first preaching assignment.

> And the seventy returned again with joy, saying, Lord, even the devils are subject unto us through thy name. (Luke 10:17)

> And he said unto them, I beheld Satan as lightning fall from Heaven. Behold, I give unto you power to tread on serpents and scorpions, and over all the power of the enemy: and nothing shall by any means hurt you. Notwithstanding in this rejoice not, that the spirits are subject unto you; but rather rejoice, because your names are written in Heaven. (Luke 10:18–20)

It was the Lord's name that the devils were subject to. But Peter and John had been sent in His name and by obeying His command, the success they had was no different than the success Christ had. This was beyond belief to the disciples the first time they experienced doing works in His Name. It is the same for all of us. When we go and do works in His name, we experience the same surprise Peter and John did when we first succeed.

But, by the time they healed the man at the gate (Acts 3:2–11), they weren't at all surprised. When Peter and John said they had been given the name, they meant that it *belonged* to them; they could use what was theirs at their discretion; they did not doubt. Doubt had been removed from the equation through a deep understanding of who they were and what they possessed from Christ. They refused to obey man and, instead, obeyed God.

However, religion demanded that they cease to preach or teach in that name. Religion was afraid that if everyone began operating as the apostles, religion would lose control of the people, and then religion would be shut down by the Roman government.

> And as they spoke unto the people, the priests and the captain of the temple, and the Sadducees came upon them, being grieved that they taught the people, and they preached through Jesus the resurrection from the dead. (Acts 4:1-2)

> And when they had set them in the midst, they asked: By what power, or by what name have ye done this? (Acts 4:7)

> Be it known unto you all, and to all the people of Israel, that by the name of Jesus Christ of Nazareth, whom ye crucified, whom God raised from the dead, even by Him doth this man stand here before you whole. This is the stone which was set at nought of you builders, which is become the head of the corner. Neither is there salvation in any other: for there is none other name under Heaven given among men, whereby we must be saved. (Acts 4:10-12)

This is the place in the story where we all jump up and shout hallelujah! But, the bigger fact of the story is that you also have been given that name. Have you laid claim to it? Have you become a possessor of that name and the power that comes with it? Will you stand against religion that can intimidate you into the yoke of control? Why allow religion to forbid you from taking ownership of what is yours?

*Accepting your appointment into the family of God with **all authority vested in Christ** is a rite of passage, a courageous stand to be who you really are. You must obey God rather than man.*

> But that it spread no further among the people, let us straightly threaten them that they speak henceforth to no man in this name. And they called them and commanded them not to speak at all, nor teach in the name of Jesus. But Peter and John answered and said unto them: Whether it be right in the sight of God to hearken unto you more than unto God, judge ye. (Acts 4:17–19)

Religion is willing to keep that name locked up within buildings made with hands, church buildings. But God has put that name in you and in me. Our testimony is threatened in the same way. Society in North America has socially engineered the people to reject Jesus; to reject His name. Peer pressure is very strong in society to restrict anyone publicly teaching or preaching in Jesus' name. His name is very powerful and invokes panic, just as it did in the religious leaders in the Temple.

I am not afraid of opposition. I have been freed by God to be bold like Peter and John. I thank my God for helping me to understand. Just because others have not understood what He has done in giving me His name, I need not speak and behave like those who lack the revelation.

I find it interesting that many will follow you when you are getting results. They, too, have eternity in their hearts. They, too, believe that they are more than religion permits. Perhaps the possibility exists that many of them will decide to break from the herd and do the works of Christ like He said they would. I work to this end. *I cannot but speak the things which I have seen and heard.*

> For we cannot but speak the things which we have seen and heard. (Acts 4:20)

Many are waking up to their call. Many have become nauseated by how powerless the body has been. We are fed up that there are so many weak and sickly among us and those who are dying before their time. It is up to *us* to fix it; stop waiting on God to come and do what He has delegated to us. He has already given us His name and all the power that goes with it.

*Let **your light** shine!*

Healing and access to healing is from God, but in the delegation or election, the responsibility of doing miracles falls to me and you as His disciples. If we don't do the works, who will? Without our cooperation and unity, the things He wishes to accomplish through us *do not* get done.

If I hide the gospel, it remains hidden from those who are lost. Because I have been given the ministry of reconciliation, I must take action that is free from any limiting beliefs or doubt. When my faith is in God and my mind is transformed to kingdom realities, I can step into the breach and fix things under the Authority of God using His wisdom and strategies. However, I must do the work. To serve Him, I must accept personal responsibility for the task.

Jesus taught personal responsibility. He told us what He expects from us, what we may expect from others when we are doing what He told us to do, and what the rewards would be for those who were willing to work.

Believing regardless of limiting beliefs and religious obstacles is easy once you break free from the lies that enslave us. When you begin to overcome the wicked one, you become empowered; you will realize that God provides the tools needed to get the job done. However, this knowledge has been withheld by those who have taken away the key of knowledge.

> Woe unto you, lawyers! For ye have taken away the key of knowledge: ye entered not in yourselves, and them that were entering in ye hindered. (Luke 11:52)

The lawyers are still among us, disempowering us by pointing us to the law as though we have not believed what Christ has said about us and our part in the kingdom. They still hinder us and in doing so, have blocked their own entrance into the kingdom. This disempowerment continues to limit us. The grave clothes of religion cause us to adopt the limitations of dead men, instead of Christ in us, the hope of glory for regenerated man. They block us from the life available to us as we abide in the vine.

Empowerment was always Christ's intent for every believer: to make capable disciples, well able to preach and to deliver the Kingdom of God with signs and wonders; disciples who are thoroughly furnished and empowered to do the works of Christ and greater.

LIE 2: ONLY GOD CAN FORGIVE SINS

> Then said Jesus to them again, Peace be unto you: as my Father hath sent me, even so send I you. And when he had said this, he breathed on them, and saith unto them, Receive ye the Holy Ghost: Whose soever sins ye remit, they are remitted unto them; and whose soever sins ye retain, they are retained. (John 20:21–23, italics mine)

Jesus forgives sins because that is what His father does and that is what His Father empowered Him to do. He then said to His disciples that they, too, would be sent in the same manner to forgive sins.

Separating us from God was what Satan did to Eve in the Garden. God said let us make man in our own image, but Satan was successful in causing Eve to believe that she was not like God. Although the truth was she was like Him, Satan's bait through deceit was to convince Eve that she needed to eat from the tree so she could become like Him and know good and evil. Satan uses the same tactic today, telling us we are not like God and that we must be good enough to merit His acceptance. Doing what He said we could do and openly declaring that we have been so empowered, has been reduced to an act of treason when nothing could be further from the truth.

When we claim to be like God, we are accused of stepping out of our place or as thinking of ourselves as being in a higher position or authority than we are entitled. But, understanding our position in Christ is the foundation for freedom from the original lie. Let us with complete courage think and say of ourselves exactly what Christ has claimed us to be. Anything short of this limits us and confusion sets in, causing us to doubt our sonship and the ability to perform the works that Christ commands us to do.

3

COMMUNION:
DISCERNING THE LORD'S PRESENCE

The gospels have no record that Jesus suffered from sickness or that He was feeble. His body served Him well. I believe He continues to desire a strong body here on Earth.

> For I have received of the Lord that which also I delivered unto you, that the Lord Jesus the same night in which he was betrayed took bread. And when he had given thanks, he broke it and said: Take, eat; this is my body, which is broken for you. Do this in remembrance of me. After the same manner he also took the cup when he had supped, saying: This cup is the new testament in my blood; this do ye as oft as ye drink it, in remembrance of me. (1 Corinthians 11:23–25)

DO THIS IN REMEMBRANCE OF ME . . .

When we fail to remember Jesus' body and blood, we stumble. It leads away from *eternal purpose* to *weakness*. Forgetting

God's eternal purpose leads us from true worship to worship in vain.

Salvation includes setting a new creature right
in every part of life.

When we forget Him, we go about to establish our own righteousness in the vanity of our minds and miss the *eternal purpose.*

But there is a *present truth* because of what Jesus did. Present truth is reality that has come about through His sacrifice. And *remembrance* causes us to be established in the present truth.

> Wherefore I will not be negligent to put you always in remembrance of these things, though ye know them, and be established in the present truth. (2 Peter 1:12)

When we remember His body that was broken for us, the fullness of His salvation permeates every part of *His life in us* and produces wholeness.

> But let a man examine himself, and so let him eat of that bread, and drink of that cup. For he that eateth and drinketh unworthily, eateth and drinketh damnation to himself, not discerning the Lord's body. For this cause many are weak and sickly among you, and many sleep. (1 Corinthians 11:28–30)

In his 1828 edition of *The American Dictionary of the English Language*, Noah Webster defines the word "unworthy" as follows.

Unworthily: anaxiōs — *an-ax-ee'-oce*

Adverb from Strongs Dictionary #G370; *irreverently: unworthily.*

The word "unworthily" in the Scripture above means irreverently, which is to approach something Holy in an unexamined or disrespectful manner.

Moses would have behaved irreverently if he had refused to take his shoes off at the burning bush, knowing that God had called it holy ground. He would have been treating the sacred as if it were trivial.

A misunderstanding of how powerful the broken body of Jesus and His shed blood are leads to weakness, sickliness and death before your time. Conversely, by examination of yourself through what has been accomplished in you because of His broken body and His shed blood, you receive *life from the dead*. This is an example of present truth; reality that has come about through His sacrifice. A reality that brings wholeness and soundness, once it is understood.

> For as often as ye eat this bread, and drink this
> cup, ye do shew the Lord's death till he come.
> (1 Corinthians 11:26)

It is by His death (and by my death in Him) that I am made alive (or He is made alive in me). In the act of Communion, I show the Lord's death until He comes.

*When I admit **my death** in Him,*
*He is **fully alive** in me.*

What would happen if we were to solemnly, reverently and soberly remember when we take communion—the broken body of Jesus, His blood shed for us—and what that means in us *as a present truth?*

Maybe the point is to not only repeat the words that Jesus spoke when He spoke of the bread and the wine; but during this time of remembrance, we could give testimony to the ways that Jesus, through His broken body, has healed our bodies—set us free—and how because of His death, **we are now remembering** how the power of His endless life means wholeness in us.

By giving our testimony, the testimony of Jesus Christ (the Spirit of Prophecy) is being released, not only making His deeds understood to all in light of the bread and the cup, but declaring that because He died entirely, we live fully. Reverently embracing His death causes life after death. He lives in us because we are dead. Communion, then, celebrates His life in us. His life quickens my mortal (dead) body. *Do I really believe that life can come from the dead?* Psalm 103 gives a practical method for acting this idea out with a group during communion.

> Bless the LORD, O my soul: and all that is within me, bless his holy name. Bless the LORD, O my soul, and forget not all his benefits: Who forgiveth all thine iniquities; who healeth all thy diseases; Who redeemeth thy life from destruction; who crowneth thee with lovingkindness and tender mercies; Who satisfieth thy mouth with good things; so that thy youth is renewed like the eagle's. The LORD executeth righteousness and judgment for all that are oppressed. (Psalm 103:1)

Read this Scripture out loud and ask that everyone focus on His benefits.

Next, ask people to give testimony of times that they have personally benefitted in these exact ways. For example, someone may give testimony of a time Jesus *delivered their lives from destruction.* Then someone else may give a testimony of Jesus' *healing them from a disease.* Then another may give testimony of how Jesus *executed judgment, saving them from an oppressive circumstance.*

I believe that if we were to approach Communion this way, the power of His death in us would release the power of an endless life, producing **wholeness** in our body as He **lives** in it. This power would eliminate the weak and sickly conditions presently hindering the full benefit of His death in me; or, to say it another way, life untouchable by death, absent of any feebleness.

> He brought them forth also with silver and gold: and there was not one feeble *person* among their tribes. (Psalm 105:37, italics mine)

Psalm 105 is a testimony of something God did for the Israelites. The Israelites remembered what He did for them. When we remember these events and retell them, it achieves two things.

1. It teaches our children the history of God's mighty acts so that they learn that He has always delivered His people and that He will deliver them, too—right now!

2. It prophetically releases deliverance through the act of declaring God's mighty deeds. In other words, His testimonies are filled with spirit and life, able to reproduce the same in all who hear them—right now!

> And I fell at his feet to worship him. And he said unto me, See thou do it not: I am thy fellow servant, and of thy brethren that have the testimony of Jesus: worship God: for the testimony of Jesus is the spirit of prophecy. (Revalation 19:10)

When testimony of Jesus is given, it creates a prophetic environment. What I mean by this, is that by giving a spoken example of how someone received the benefits of His broken body or His shed blood, we open a door for the same grace to be present that caused the freedom within these individual lives. The power of the words of the testimony releases the power of God to heal in the moment. Perhaps the best person to bring healing to another is the *one testifying* of the freedom they received.

The testimony from the *one healed* releases the *power of the Lord to heal.* The testimony of the *one Jesus delivered* from destruction releases the *power of the Lord to deliver* those who need the same freedom. The testimony of the *one freed from oppression* releases the *power of the Lord to free captives* held in oppressive ways, or by the oppression of the devil.

This kind of testimony turns a non-eventful ceremony into a prophetic remembrance, releasing the power to deliver those who are weak, sickly or about ready to die among us. This is entering into present truth.

By prophetic remembrance, we draw the power to overcome bodily conditions that are subject to change from the kingdom within.

Remembrance is done purposely. The Apostle Peter knew the importance of remembering.

> This second epistle, beloved, I now write unto you; in both which I stir up your pure minds by way of remembrance. (2 Peter 3:1)

> Wherefore I will not be negligent to put you always in remembrance of these things, though ye know them, and be established in the present truth. Yea, I think it meet, as long as I am in this tabernacle, to stir you up by putting you in remembrance. (2 Peter 1:12–13)

Re-member-ing The House of Israel

The hand of the LORD was upon me, and carried me out in the spirit of the LORD, and set me down in the midst of the valley which was full of bones, and caused me to pass by them round about; and, behold, there were very many in the open valley; and, lo, they were very dry. (Ezekiel 37:1-2)

And he said unto me, Son of man, can these bones live? And I answered, O Lord GOD, thou knowest. Again he said unto me, Prophesy upon these bones, and say unto them, O ye dry bones, hear the word of the LORD. Thus saith the LORD GOD unto these bones; Behold, I will cause breath to enter into you, and ye shall live: And I will lay sinews upon you, and will bring up flesh upon you, and cover you with skin, and put breath in you, and ye shall live; and ye shall know that I am the LORD. So I prophesied as I was commanded: and as I prophesied, there was a noise, and behold a shaking, and the bones came together, bone to his bone. And when I beheld, lo, the sinews and the flesh came up upon them, and the skin covered them above: but there was no breath in them.

Then said he unto me, Prophesy unto the wind, prophesy, son of man, and say to the wind, Thus saith the Lord GOD; Come from the four winds, O breath, and breathe upon these slain, that they may live. So I prophesied as he commanded me, and the breath came into them, and they lived, and stood up upon their feet, an exceeding great army. Then he said unto me, Son of man, these bones are the whole

> house of Israel: behold, they say, Our bones are dried, and our hope is lost: we are cut off for our parts. Therefore prophesy and say unto them, Thus saith the LORD GOD; Behold, O my people, I will open your graves, and cause you to come up out of your graves, and bring you into the land of Israel. (Ezekiel 37:3–12)

Dry bones are brittle. The bones described in Ezekiel had been the remnants of slaughter—slain men—some probably without limbs and/or heads; they were laying there until nothing remained but bones left to bake in the sun for years.

God asked Ezekiel if these dry brittle bones can live. Ezekiel's response was, essentially, *You tell me God*, as he didn't know. So God instructs Ezekiel: "**Prophesy upon these bones, and say unto them, O ye dry bones, hear the word of the Lord. Thus saith the Lord God unto these bones; Behold, I will cause breath to enter into you, and ye shall live**" (Ezekiel 37:4–5).

When heard, the word of the Lord will cause a response. **But does a bone have an ear?** It doesn't matter. If God says bones can hear, they can hear. If He can make a rock cry out, He can make a bone hear.

Have you ever talked to a bone? I have.

God said to the bones: "**I will cause breath to enter into you, and ye shall live.**" As Ezekiel prophesied, the bones began to come together, attaching each one to the other, in place from the places they fell. They came together forming complete skeletons, then all the connecting tissue and sinews, then flesh and skin for a covering. Yet they had no breath in them.

Ezekiel watched the whole valley of bones re-attach to each other before his eyes. Imagine Ezekiel's thoughts as he watched this miracle occur. But God wasn't finished. Because they had no breath in them, God then commanded Ezekiel to prophecy to the breath. What? *Prophesy to the breath?*

> Then said he unto me, Prophesy unto the wind,
> prophesy, son of man, and say to the wind,
> Thus saith the Lord GOD; Come from the four
> winds, O breath, and breathe upon these slain,
> that they may live. So I prophesied as he com-
> manded me, and the breath came into them,
> and they lived, and stood up upon their feet, an
> exceeding great army. (Ezekiel 37:9–10)

An army emerges; an exceedingly great army.

Noah Webster (1828) lists two definitions for the word "member":

Member: n. [Fr. *membre*; L. *membrum*]

The first definition of member is **a subordinate part of the main body, such as a leg, an arm, an ear, or a finger.**

Ezekiel watched God re-*member*-ing body parts—*re-attaching them back to the bodies* and then *bringing to them everything that is required to be alive again,* including breath.

In my experience, I've found that working miracles requires unusual thinking. It requires meditating on unusual levels; seeing things from a perspective you have not imagined before. The challenge is to stay impregnated with inspiration from the unseen realm where anything is possible, making room for the unknown to manifest. This is like preparing a nursery for a baby that you know is coming. The baby is on the way, you are making ready and bringing together what is needed.

If I believe that anything can happen at any given time, I allow myself to see things in unusual ways. I give the Kingdom of God a very wide berth. When the kingdom comes (as we have been praying for two thousand years), His will is done. Often, it is unexpected and unusual. When you position yourself for miracles, expecting them at all times, they happen all the time.

Like Ezekiel learned, I know now that although I may not have seen something before, it doesn't mean that it's impossible for that something to occur. As we set our affections on things above, we position ourselves to be a gateway to Heaven for His kingdom to manifest outward from within us. We release miracles from the kingdom within, where God dwells. What would happen if we gave Him absolute freedom to move as He pleases? He will activate the visionary potential of our imagination to see into an unseen realm, just like He did for Ezekiel.

When that happens, we are then able to pull a visible miracle out from an invisible realm; we will work miracles. We arrive on the scene with an impregnated imagination saturated with Heaven's prophetic potential. The miracle *is being birthed* in real time, *crowning at just the right moment—when suddenly,* there's *the Baby!* Now you see it!

I look at a missing leg thinking, *can that leg grow out? What would that look like? It looks like it's missing—but is it really missing? God, is it missing from your sight, or do you see a leg there? If you had your way with me; if there were no unbelief in me, could this missing leg be un-missing? Yay God! What would you have me do?*

> *I am willing to look like a fool to the world*
> *if it pleases Heaven.*

What is the cloud of witnesses doing at this moment? Is there an ancestor of this person with the missing leg agreeing with you and God for a miracle right now? Is this person seeking God for a new leg? Would you like it if I offered to pray for them, Lord? Is this the moment that I get to see a leg grow out? Are you still in the business of re-member-ing bodies, as Ezekiel witnessed you do? If you are, let's go.

There may not be many people thinking this way. There may not be many people praying for such manifestations. Jesus had these manifestations; He must have thought about making people whole. He said we would do these things and greater, if we believed. Where's the disconnect? Where are the believing ones?

How come the gap between the prophetic declaration and our attention to it is so far apart?

Remembering the testimonies of Jesus and declaring them prophetically as present-day realities may be where the gap exists. What if we are so close to making the miraculous the rule and not the exception to the rule?

Noah Webster's 1828 dictionary tells us that "re-member-ing" means **restoring members, limbs, organs, and body parts.**

Remembering causes us to understand Jesus' acts. His acts were restorative; He came to bring the mountains low, to make the crooked places straight: making wrongs right, repairing the breach, and destroying the enmity.

By not remembering, *what was done for us fades from our memory and from our testimony.* Instead, by remembrance, *we intentionally keep what He has done for us in our hearts, our minds, and in our mouths.* In this way, we are impregnated with miracle-working power and divine inspiration. We are able to release the power, fully expecting the one who never changes to blast all feebleness, sickness and premature death from our midst.

Can these bones live? Bones, members of individual bodies, lying in a heap were re-member-ed, reattached. Bones came back into place, sinews of flesh and muscles—re-man-tled—*re-membered.* Praise God!

Perhaps we can re-member Jesus in every place where His body is now fragmented, out of place, or has members missing. Communion is bringing the wholeness back to the body. Jesus broke the bread and gave it to His disciples. Communion is the bread coming back together, remembering that we were made whole because of the broken body and shed blood of Jesus Christ.

The second definition of "member" is **an individual member of a community or society.**

A dis-membered body or group of people is a group dysfunctional, broken apart, disorganized, and lacking in mobilization or in the ability to function in healthy ways.

> Then he said unto me: Son of man, these bones are the whole house of Israel; behold, they say, "Our bones are dried, and our hope is lost; we are cut off for our parts." (Ezekiel 37:11)

Hopelessness—dryness of the bones.

> A merry heart doeth good like a medicine: but a broken spirit drieth the bones. (Proverbs 17:22)

Through hopelessness, Israel was experiencing dry bones. They had become fragmented, disjointed due to hopelessness—*a broken spirit.*

> A merry heart maketh a cheerful countenance: but by sorrow of the heart the spirit is broken. (Proverbs 15:13)

> He that hath no rule over his own spirit is like a city that is broken down, and without walls. (Proverbs 25:28)

There are many who can relate with Israel, as there are many weak and sickly among us, and some even sleep. But our body, the body of Christ can be made whole. Our dry bones can and will live. We will prophetically re-member and build from our dry bones an exceedingly great army. We are able to rightly discern the Lord's body, restoring our fallen brethren, who will join us as we become a great army.

Jesus has already given us the prophetic image of this army through the prophets. We previously looked at Ezekiel in regards to Israel. As Christians, we must keep in mind that we have been grafted into spiritual Israel.

In addition, the Church of Christ is also prophetically distinctive. The Church is foretold in prophecy under the names of *Zion* and the *holy mountain (the stone cut out without hands), which became a great mountain and filled the whole Earth.*

> Thou sawest till that a stone was cut out without hands, which smote the image upon his feet that were of iron and clay, and brake them to pieces. Then was the iron, the clay, the brass, the silver, and the gold, broken to pieces together, and became like the chaff of the summer threshing-floors; and the wind carried them away, that no place was found for them: and the stone that smote the image became a great mountain, and filled the whole Earth. (Daniel 2:34–35)

> Blow ye the trumpet in Zion, and sound an alarm in my holy mountain: let all the inhabitants of the land tremble: for the day of the LORD cometh, for it is nigh at hand; A day of darkness and of gloominess, a day of clouds and of thick darkness, as the morning spread upon the mountains: a great people and a strong; there hath not been ever the like, neither shall be any more after it, even to the years of many generations. A fire devoureth before them; and behind them a flame burneth: the land is as the garden of Eden before them, and behind them a desolate wilderness; yea, and nothing shall escape them.
>
> The appearance of them is as the appearance of horses; and as horsemen, so shall they

run. Like the noise of chariots on the tops of mountains shall they leap, like the noise of a flame of fire that devoureth the stubble, as a strong people set in battle array. Before their face the people shall be much pained: all faces shall gather blackness. They shall run like mighty men; they shall climb the wall like men of war; and they shall march every one on his ways, and they shall not break their ranks: Neither shall one thrust another; they shall walk every one in his path: and when they fall upon the sword, they shall not be wounded. They shall run to and fro in the city; they shall run upon the wall, they shall climb up upon the houses; they shall enter in at the windows like a thief.

The Earth shall quake before them; the Heavens shall tremble: the sun and the moon shall be dark, and the stars shall withdraw their shining: And the LORD shall utter his voice before his army: for his camp is very great: for he is strong that executeth his word: for the day of the LORD is great and very terrible; and who can abide it? (Joel 2:1–11)

This Scripture refers to a great army described as

- a strong and great people;
- unprecedented in historical remembrance;
- unrepeated in the future; and
- a strong people set in battle array.

This is a powerful army where

- a fire devours before them—a flame burns behind them;
- the land is as the garden of Eden before them—and behind them a desolate wilderness;
- nothing escapes them;
- they each march in their own path;
- they don't break their ranks;
- they don't hurt each other;
- they are immune to the weapons used against them; and
- the Earth quakes and the Heavens tremble before them.

This is a mighty army that

- has the appearance of horses, powerfully running;
- leaps like the noise of chariots upon the mountain tops;
- is like the noise of a flame of fire that devours the stubble;
- runs like mighty men; and
- scales walls like men of war.

The great army described in Scripture is a description of the Church. This is who we are as we remember and rightly discern the Lord's body. As Jesus builds His church, it becomes a mighty mountain that covers the whole Earth. It breaks the clay and iron feet of the image in Daniel's vision and it comes crumbling to the Earth like the chaff of the summer threshing floor. The wind carried the pieces of his vision away and no place was found for them.

But, all the parts of these dry bones come back together into an exceedingly great army that covers the Earth.

This is our destiny—this is who we are—it is written;
therefore, it will happen.
It is a work of God.

When the prophetic timetable has aligned with His decree, the breath will come from the four winds and cause the divine life, and the greatness thereof to emerge. There is a fulfillment of this in the Book of Psalms.

> My heart is smitten, and withered like grass; so that I forget to eat my bread. By reason of the voice of my groaning my bones cleave to my skin. I am like a pelican of the wilderness: I am like an owl of the desert. I watch, and am as a sparrow alone upon the house top. Mine enemies reproach me all the day; and they that are mad against me are sworn against me. For I have eaten ashes like bread, and mingled my drink with weeping, Because of thine indignation and thy wrath: for thou hast lifted me up, and cast me down.
>
> My days are like a shadow that declineth; and I am withered like grass. But thou, O LORD, shalt endure for ever; and thy remembrance unto all generations. Thou shalt arise, and have mercy upon Zion: for the time to favour her, yea, the set time, is come. For thy servants take pleasure in her stones, and favour the dust thereof. So the heathen shall fear the name of the LORD, and all the kings of the Earth thy glory. When the LORD shall build up Zion, he shall appear in his glory. (Psalm 102:4–16)

There is a set time to favor Zion—when the Lord shall arise in His mercy. When the set time comes, the Lord will appear in His glory. He will tabernacle in His Shekinah glory within His church—the temple of the Holy Ghost.

As in the dry bones, Psalm 102 reveals that Israel had lost hope:

- My heart is smitten and withered like grass so that I forget to eat

- My bones cleave to my skin by reason of my groanings

- My eating is of ashes for bread

- My tears mingle in my drink

- My days are like a shadow that declineth

God's servants take pleasure in the stones and favour the dust thereof. No matter what life brings, we have hope because God is faithful to do what He says. When hope seems lost, He revives us. We may become cast down at times, but we are not forsaken. We are never abandoned to walk alone. He is at work within us. Suffering has its place in our walk and does a work in us. When we fellowship in His sufferings, we know him better, because He also suffered for us. We bear in our bodies the marks of the Lord Jesus. We endure the same things He did. We are touched, because like Him, we have experienced trials and have endured.

> For we have not an high priest which cannot
> be touched with the feeling of our infirmities;
> but was in all points tempted like as we are, yet
> without sin. (Hebrews 4:15)

In addition to the suffering and testing, He has called us to re-member His body. We carry out the prophetic destiny of bringing wholeness. We will succeed because it is written. God always has the last say. When He has built us (Zion) up He will appear in His glory. He will completely inhabit us in His full strength.

There is an army being built up, strengthened and in ever-increasing ways, we are being deployed to restore members to the body that have fallen away and have become like the dry bones in Ezekiel's vision. You and I are privileged to be involved in this great restoration. *Praise God!*

> *Did you realize yet that you are the wind*
> *that brings the breath?*

> Jesus answered, Verily, verily, I say unto thee, Except a man be born of water and of the Spirit, he cannot enter into the Kingdom of God. That which is born of the flesh is flesh; and that which is born of the Spirit is spirit. Marvel not that I said unto thee, Ye must be born again. The wind bloweth where it listeth, and thou hearest the sound thereof, but canst not tell whence it cometh, and whither it goeth: so is every one that is born of the Spirit. (John 3:5–8)

We have been born by His spirit as the wind; not seen, we manifest His glory. Like the wind, which rustles the leaves and brings physical evidence of its existence, we also blow in and blow away. But as we touch the slain, they raise up, becoming whole by the breath of the almighty as they are healed and restored. They are raised up to become a mighty army, capable of deployment and single-minded in purpose.

Body parts are needed. They are stored for you as you blow by the slain, downcast, wounded and fallen. Grab as many body parts as you can.

4

ABRAHAM'S
UNCHANGEABLE BLESSING

A braham gave a tenth of the spoils gained by defeating the kings who attacked Sodom and other cities. The kings had taken Lot and all his possessions captive.

> And Melchizedek, king of Salem, brought forth bread and wine; and he was the priest of the most high God. And he blessed him, and said: Blessed be Abram of the most high God, possessor of Heaven and Earth. And blessed be the most high God, which hath delivered thine enemies into thy hand. And he gave him tithes of all. (Genesis 14:18–20)

In the Book of Hebrews, there is an interesting passage concerning this meeting with Melchizedek.

> For Melchisedec, king of Salem, priest of the most high God, who met Abraham returning from the slaughter of the kings and blessed him; to whom also Abraham gave a tenth part

of all; first being by interpretation king of righteousness, and after that also king of Salem, which is, king of peace; without father, without mother, without descent, having neither beginning of days, nor end of life, but made like unto the Son of God; abideth a priest continually.

Now consider how great this man was, unto whom even the patriarch Abraham gave the tenth of the spoils. And verily they that are of the sons of Levi, who receive the office of the priesthood, have a commandment to take tithes of the people according to the law, that is, of their brethren, though they come out of the loins of Abraham. But he whose descent is not counted from them received tithes of Abraham, and blessed him that had the promises. And without all contradiction the less is blessed of the better. And here men that die receive tithes; but there he receiveth them, of whom it is witnessed that he liveth.

And as I may so say, *Levi also, who receiveth tithes, payed tithes in Abraham. For he was yet in the loins of his father when Melchisedec met him.* If, therefore, perfection were by the Levitical priesthood, (for under it the people received the law,) what further need was there that another priest should rise after the order of Melchisedec, and not be called after the order of Aaron? For the priesthood being changed, there is made of necessity a change also of the law. For He of whom these things are spoken, pertaineth to another tribe, of which no man gave attendance at the altar. For it is evident that our Lord sprang out of Juda; of which tribe Moses spake nothing concerning priesthood.

And it is yet far more evident; for that after the similitude of Melchisedec, there ariseth another priest, Who is made, not after the law of a carnal commandment, but after the power of an endless life. For he testifieth, Thou art a priest for ever after the order of Melchisedec. For there is verily a disannulling of the commandment going before for the weakness and unprofitableness thereof. For the law made nothing perfect, but the bringing in of a better hope did; by which we draw nigh unto God. (Hebrews 7:1–19, italics mine)

These Scriptures contrast the Melchizedek priesthood with the Levitical priesthood. The book of Hebrews points out that although Levi was commanded under the law to receive tithes from the people, his own tithes were already paid while he was in the loins of his father, Abraham. There were many generations between Abraham and Levi, yet God speaks of that day—the day Abraham paid all tithes off, once and for all.

The tithe was paid for all in the order of Melchizedek. This means that when I receive Christ, I come into the family of God where *tithes of all* were paid in Abraham. In Christ, the law is fulfilled. It was His body and blood, the bread and the wine, which Abram partook of that day. From an unchangeable priesthood, my tithes were declared paid in Abraham.

At the change of priesthoods (from the Levitical to the Melchizedek in Christ), *the commandment to tithe was disannulled.* There was no perfection in the law, but a better hope changed everything. It is in Christ that the Gentiles have become Abraham's seed. As his seed, our tithes were paid the day Melchizedek received a *tenth of all,* just like Levi's had been. Not only was the law of the tithe disannulled, but the entire law. If we keep even part of the law, we are responsible to keep the whole thing.

For whosoever shall keep the whole law, and yet offend in one point, he is guilty of all. For he that said do not commit adultery, said also, do not kill. Now if thou commit no adultery, yet if thou kill, thou art become a transgressor of the law. So speak ye and so do as they that shall be judged by the law of liberty. (James 2:10–12 mine)

Know ye therefore that they which are of faith, the same are the children of Abraham. And the scripture, foreseeing that God would justify the heathen through faith, preached before the gospel unto Abraham, sayingi In thee shall all nations be blessed. So then, they which be of faith are blessed with faithful Abraham. For as many as are of the works of the law are under the curse; for it is written, Cursed is every one that continueth not in all things which are written in the book of the law to do them. But that no man is justified by the law in the sight of God, it is evident; for the just shall live by faith. And the law is not of faith: but, the man that doeth them shall live in them. (Galatians 3:7–12)

Because we are liberated from living under the law through Faith in Jesus Christ, we are justified in Him, and the *just* shall live by faith. Even though we have been freed from the law, there has been a centralized system of financial control in the church. Rather than teach New Testament stewardship and the use of one's finances to finance creative individual and family exploits, the church became a management company. It formed a board of directors that would decide how to steward the people's money for them. This has had the effect of centralizing assets. The financial power of many is now controlled by a few.

Personal stewardship is taught in the context of how you manage what's left over after God has removed *His cut* from your budget. The implied message is that as a new creation, you cannot be trusted to steward what God has put into your hands, but you are expected to comply with the traditions of the church and to never question why you *have to*. Slaves have no choice, but a new creation does. This is not taught in the Church. Jesus taught it, but it has been largely abandoned by the organized church in favor of the power to control other people's money; building from the labors of many, what the few have decided is best. Corporate church structure steals the provision of individuals, which would otherwise facilitate individual and family outreach endeavors.

One example of this is a family who brings all their tithes and offerings into *the storehouse* (Old Testament). The family did not pursue individual and family callings because they weren't taught self-actualization. They were not let in on the notion that each of us has a ministry that will require individual assets to accomplish.

ARMED ROBBERY

I recently sat through a terrible example of manipulation for an offering for a visiting prophet. The pastor used an Old Testament Scripture out of context that he said promised a blessing.

> There is that scattereth and yet increaseth; and there is that withholdeth more than is meet, but it tendeth to poverty. The liberal soul shall be made fat, and he that watereth shall be watered also himself. (Proverbs 11:24-25)

He suggested that those who resisted giving into the offering were operating under a religious spirit and that he could perceive their resistance. He then talked about the ones who were thinking that if they gave, they would not be able to meet their obligations at home, and in so doing, did not have faith in

God. He suggested that they were attracting poverty by resisting giving into this offering.

He spoke about this for approximately 15 minutes, and then he finally took up the offering. I was looking at the faces in the crowd; I noticed many had their resistance broken down after being labeled so negatively and insulted by this pastor.

I was saddened to hear him promise that within 21 days there would be testimonies of supernatural provision from many who gave *sacrificially*. I felt sorry for the people who would go back home with their pockets picked by such nonsense; their own assets stolen through spiritual graft. Perhaps *witch-graft* would better describe such a shameless misuse of one's position (graft, meaning *the unscrupulous use of one's authority for personal gain*).

Brethren, these things ought not be so. Assets in the kingdom are a means to an end.

> And he said also unto his disciples: There was a certain rich man, who had a steward, and the same was accused unto him that he had wasted his goods. And he called him, and said unto him: How is it that I hear this of thee? Give an account of thy stewardship, for thou mayest be no longer steward. Then the steward said within himself: What shall I do? For my lord taketh away from me the stewardship; I cannot dig, to beg I am ashamed. I am resolved what to do; that, when I am put out of the stewardship, they may receive me into their houses.
>
> So he called every one of his lord's debtors unto him, and said unto the first: How much owest thou unto my lord? And he said: A hundred measures of oil. And he said unto him: Take thy bill and sit down quickly, and write fifty. Then said he to another: And how much owest thou? And he said, A hundred measures

of wheat. And he said unto him: Take thy bill and write fourscore. And the lord commended the unjust steward, because he had done wisely; for the children of this world are in their generation wiser than the children of light.

And I say unto you: Make to yourselves friends of the mammon of unrighteousness; that, when ye fail, they may receive you into everlasting habitations. He that is faithful in that which is least, is faithful also in much; and he that is unjust in the least, is unjust also in much. If therefore, ye have not been faithful in the unrighteous mammon, who will commit to your trust the true riches? And if ye have not been faithful in that which is another man's, who shall give you that which is your own? No servant can serve two masters; for either he will hate the one, and love the other; or else, he will hold to the one, and despise the other. Ye cannot serve God and mammon.

And the Pharisees also, who were covetous, heard all these things, and they derided him. And he said unto them: Ye are they which justify yourselves before men, but God knoweth your hearts; for that which is highly esteemed among men is abomination in the sight of God. The law and the prophets were until John; since that time the Kingdom of God is preached, and every man presseth into it. (Luke 16:1–16)

The teaching in Luke was to every man. The law was on its way out. The waste caused from the perverse stewardship of the Pharisees was being confronted by Jesus. The Pharisees, who were covetous, were furious about Jesus' teachings concerning *the de-centralization of financial control* (Pharisees in charge of the money). Stewardship of financial provision was being changed under a new priesthood. Stewardship was to become an *individual calling*.

> And the Pharisees also, who were covetous,
> heard all these things and they derided him.
> (Luke 16:14)

Every man would now be expected to properly steward the mammon of unrighteousness, converting it into a means of debt cancellation; winning the lost, cancelling the debts of men, pressing into the kingdom.

While corporate vision and focus are necessary in the kingdom, they cannot be more important than personal stewardship. The *mammon* would be subject to the *individual discretion* of sons. Each person would become responsible for individual stewardship. The Pharisees were not warm to Jesus' treatise on kingdom finance. Decentralization of financial power was not what they wanted to hear. The Pharisees were livid. The love of money had become the evil means of controlling the people; manipulating them and abusing them.

Corporate religion still does not want to yield to the Lord in this, but continues to drive the people back under the law using Scriptures that were written while the people were under the law of Moses and under a different priesthood. Corporate religion controls the people's money and wastes significant amounts of it, just like the Pharisees had. The people's money that Jesus earmarked for their personal and family ministry has been hijacked and used by the corporate system.

> Woe unto you scribes and Pharisees, you hypocrites! For ye devour widows' houses, and for a pretense make long prayer; therefore, ye shall receive the greater damnation. (Matthew 23:14)

This did not deter the scribes and Pharisees in their mastery of taking up an offering. They were good at it. They filled the treasuries with unjustifiable gain at the expense of the poor and needy. They did this over and above the scriptural mandates, and through this, oppressed the people.

There is not a single reference in the law requiring widows to tithe. Poor widows were to be provided for under the law, not to be exploited. No wonder Jesus spoke to religious leaders like He did. He was putting a stop to this system of religion and bringing in something better.

You may find the debt cancellation in this teaching confusing, unless you realize that the rich man in this lesson is God himself. The stewards were the Pharisees, who if wise, would concede that their stewardship was ending and befriend those set free from the law. Jesus was cancelling the debts of the whole world. In so doing, the financial power structures would end as a corporate instrument of stealing from the people, at least within His kingdom. Jesus was handing them their walking papers.

While under the law, those in debt are slaves to it. But the rich man was after sons. His goal was to convert slaves into sons. Sons are free from the old system. They no longer have debts to God. This means that tithing and the centralization of God's money would be a thing of the past. Under the law, if you did not pay your tithes, you were *robbing God* and were cursed; but when you follow Jesus into the regeneration, you become God's son and have no debt any more. God has cancelled your entire debt to bring *tithes into the storehouse.*

The business of God was no longer going to be a centralized system that governed slaves, but a family of sons who have tremendous potential for individual and collective greatness, while stewardship of personal assets remain within their control. The idea of children freed from the old system of tithing and paying temple tax is highlighted again by Jesus when Peter told him that they were being required to pay tribute (tax) money.

> And when they were come to Capernaum, they
> that received tribute money came to Peter,

> and said, Doth not your master pay tribute?
> He saith, Yes. And when he was come into
> the house, Jesus prevented him, saying, What
> thinkest thou, Simon? of whom do the kings of
> the earth take custom or tribute? of their own
> children, or of strangers? Peter saith unto him,
> Of strangers. Jesus saith unto him, Then are the
> children free. (Mathew 17:24-26)

We who believe enter into a family that has been made free, and we now have the joy of hearing from God ourselves. We understand who we are and what belongs to us as sons and daughters when we *press into the Kingdom.* Now we are free to steward our money in more productive ways as Jesus, who is the head, leads us. God has faith in His sons and daughters to choose for ourselves how best to use the mammon of unrighteousness to further the kingdom. A kingdom blueprint emerges as we shed the slave garments; coming out from under the curse and getting comfortable wearing our royal family garments.

Furthering the kingdom is not best decided by the board of a local church, but by individuals pressing into the kingdom, seeking God as to the individual and family ministries they are called to.

I am not saying that giving into a church body is wrong. It is clear that Paul took offerings laid up for the poor saints at Jerusalem. They did not do this out of compulsion nor were they manipulated, but God himself was moving upon them to use assets *as means of loving one another.*

> But a certain man named Ananias with Sap-
> phira his wife, sold a possession and kept back
> part of the price, his wife also being privy to
> it, and brought a certain part and laid it at the
> apostles' feet. But Peter said: Ananias, why hath
> Satan filled thine heart to lie to the Holy Ghost,

and to keep back part of the price of the land?
Whiles it remained, *was it not thine own?* And
after it was sold, *was it not in thine own power?*
Why hast thou conceived this thing in thine
heart? Thou hast not lied unto men, but unto
God. (Acts 5:1–4, italics mine)

In Acts 4, many who owned land and houses sold them and
brought the proceeds to the apostles which were laid at their
feet. A distribution was made so that everyone had what they
needed. This was done of their own free will from their own
assets without a requirement to do so.

To see the wisdom of this grace upon them, we should
note that nowhere does it say that these people sold everything
they owned. The balance was in those having more than they
required sell some of their possessions to provide for those
who were in need; not that those who were rich became poor.

Ananias and Sapphira had a different take on this. They
wished to be known amongst those who sold and gave, but
their hearts were filled by Satan to lie to the Holy Ghost. They
conspired to lie about the price of the sale by keeping back part
of the price, while pretending to give it all.

Now, read what Peter said to them about who controlled
the money.

Whiles it remained, was it not *thine own?* And
after it was sold, was it not in *thine own power?*
(Acts 5:4, italics mine)

This money did not belong to God; it belonged to Ananias
and Sapphira. Even after they sold it, the proceeds still belonged
to them. The apostles laid no claim to the money. It was not to
further their ministry, and was not asked for; instead, the people saw a need and developed a strategy to meet it.

Church finance had been de-centralized. No Longer were
slaves bringing in a mandatory tithe or offering, but sons were

stewarding their own money. Ananias and Sapphira were behaving as slaves when they believed they were under obligation; hiding their dealings to keep a little back for themselves. Peter was baffled by their approach and spoke the truth; they were not required to do anything. Their property was in their power. Satan had deceived them, filling their hearts with the mind-set of slaves under the law.

When you are discerning the Lord's body, any belief that causes you to live as though Jesus did not free you from the law can cause dysfunction in your mental, emotional and physical health. The law brings us under bondage and obligation. We are free from the law; but if we live as though we are still under the law, it brings a curse.

> For he that eateth and drinketh unworthily, eateth and drinketh damnation to himself, not discerning the Lord's body. For this cause, many are weak and sickly among you, and many sleep. (1 Corinthians 11:29–30)

As Jesus' broken body hung on the cross, He became our curse. When we own that realization, we cannot be cursed. But, if instead we begin to do those things that the law requires, we live as though Jesus' sacrifice was in vain. We partake of the Lord's Supper not understanding what we have been freed from. The power available in remembering the Lord's death till He comes misses us. This is why so many are weak and sickly among us and many sleep. The *damnation* that we eat and drink to ourselves is a curse of the law.

If you are paying tithes under a sense of obligation, you are back under the law. If the clergy teaches that *the tithe is still for today*, they may as well finish the sentence by saying *you are required to keep the whole law*. But, when you keep the law, you are under the curse of the law. No believer in Christ is subject to the law, unless they agree to keep it. In keeping any part of the law, they live as though they are not justified in Christ and reject the faith. They are returned to slavery.

THE CLERGY CONSPIRACY

In an article entitled "The Seven Worst (and Best) Things I did in Traditional Church Ministry," Pastor Smith writes this about two of his worst:

> **Took a full-time salary.** Until I left the ministry, I had no idea how corrupting a compensation package is to the church. It changes the way you think about yourself and changes the way people view you. You become a sort of professional Christian that floats above the unwashed masses of laity. It affects your decision-making almost every day. The Trinity becomes Father, Son and Holy Cash Flow.

> **Defended tithing as a principle.** This is closely related to the first point. By "defended," I mean that I never really believed that tithing was a New Testament requirement, but I kept the clergy conspiracy of silence in order to protect the finances of the church. By "principle" I mean a nicer word for "law." No one in our congregation had to tithe, but if they wanted to be in any leadership role—well . . .

Tithing can interfere with son-ship, faith and having prayers answered; tithing can expose you to the curse of the law causing health, financial, marital and many other problems.

Living under a curse is very stressful. Torment is a way of life; no matter how much you try, you never live up to the law's requirements. Living under this stress, weakens people. It causes them to become sickly and kills them before their time.

DISEASE

The word "disease" means *not at ease; not at peace; not at rest*. Awareness that you have been set at liberty through Christ, brings you into a state of rest. This is the way to take Communion worthily. You are remembering that Jesus did everything needed to satisfy the requirements of the law. This means there is nothing for you to do but thank Him and enter into rest by faith.

When Abraham took communion with Melchizedek, he entered into rest. God made him a promise that he had nothing to do with performing. God would do everything required to keep His promise to Abraham.

Sympathetic Nervous System

The sympathetic nervous system controls the release of stress hormones to give us a burst of energy and fast reflexes. These stress hormones include adrenaline, cortisol, and norepinephrine. Stress can lead to changes in the serum level of many hormones including glucocorticoids, catecholamines, growth hormone and prolactin. Some of these changes are necessary for the fight or flight response to protect oneself. However, long term changes in serum levels are believed to disrupt the stability of healthy cell tissues in the body. This *dis-ease* of normal function causes weakness and breakdown of our health.

Prolonged or continuous release of stress hormones creates chaos in all of our body systems and can confuse our immune system to attack good cells instead of bad ones. This attack on the immune system is an autoimmune disorder. Lupus is one example of many autoimmune disorders.

The sympathetic nervous system acts as a temporary response that releases hormones when energy or rapid reflexes are necessary. Therefore, it does not function continuously. Exercise is an appropriate functioning of the sympathetic nervous system and has a benefit. The *inappropriate function* of the sympathetic nervous system during stress creates undue strain on the body.

When a person endures stress on a regular basis, the sympathetic nervous system continuously releases stress hormones, which can lead to numerous health problems including heart conditions, nervous disorders, digestive problems, and sleep disorders. Stress is by far the number one killer in the world today.

When Jesus asks us to forgive, He is helping us to be in harmony. Forgiveness frees us from the bitterness that causes us to be stressful. Worry leads to stress. When Jesus said take no thought for tomorrow, He was addressing the worry and anxiety that leads to stress disorders, heart conditions, sleeplessness and other things that weaken us, cause us to become sick, and to die prematurely.

When our bodies function on the sympathetic nervous system, the indicators are a racing heart, anxiety, and shortness of breath. During exercise, the sympathetic nervous system operates in a healthy way, and stress is released. However, stress hormones can be addictive. Some create chaos because they are addicted to the feelings of stress hormones and cannot stand just resting and being calm. We are able to handle such internal abuse for a time, but eventually our systems begin to show signs of disease; weakness, sickness, and premature death. The toxic effects from the continuous release of stress hormones can have serious consequences on our health.

Parasympathetic Nervous System

Under the Parasympathetic nervous system, our bodies are relaxed and our breathing is slow and deep. This is the state of rest and balance where all our body systems operate in harmony. Our bodies are at peace. In this state, the immune system operates as it should, and fights anything within the body that is not friendly.

When we understand that Jesus entered into rest at the right hand of the Father and that we have been raised together with him and made to sit together with him in heavenly places, we can enter this state of rest.

> For he that is entered into his rest, he also hath ceased from his own works, as God did from his. Let us labour therefore to enter into that rest, lest any man fall after the same example of unbelief. (Hebrews 4:10–11)

Unbelief drives us to live as though we are still under the curse; faith causes us to enter into His rest, therefore ceasing from our own labors as Christ has from his. This position is one of great power, because we operate at peace in an absence of stress, worry and striving. Keeping the law causes the opposite.

GIVING UP THE CURSE

Remembering the body and blood of Jesus is a return to the revelation that anything needed to bring you out from under the law and the curse of the law was accomplished through the cross of Christ. Anything short of this complete freedom leaves you operating as a slave.

Instead of keeping the law, put a royal ring on your finger, a royal robe around you, and a crown on your head, because keeping the law causes you to remain living in the servant's quarters instead of in the palace where you belong.

THE YEAR OF JUBILEE

Christ would later come and cancel all the debts, restoring what rightfully belonged to Abraham and his descendants. His broken Body would grant access to that which is beyond the veil. The veil is taken away in Christ, who is a priest forever, after the order of Melchizedek. This is unlike the Levitical priesthood, which had to make atonement for the sins of the people continually. This new priest from Judah would offer for the sins of the people once and only once. There was no need for any further sacrifice for sin. This was the jubilee, an acceptable year of the Lord, where the entire debt for the sins of the people would be paid in full, once and for all. They would go free from the carnal commandments, which included tithing.

The entire debt of Adam would be cancelled by the shed blood of Christ, and His broken body would cancel the enmity between God and man. This act brought peace and restored righteousness for all who would believe on Christ. Freedom from the law of sin and death was brought about by the law of the Spirit of life in Christ Jesus; the dead children of Adam would become the children of God. A new creation is birthed in this exchange by the broken Body and the shed blood. To drink His blood and eat His flesh is to receive life from the dead.

> And you hath he quickened, who were dead in trespasses and sins. (Ephesians 2:1)

The Jubilee Manifests in Kogi State, Nigeria

While in Nigeria, I ministered to Muslims for the first time. After a morning training session for leaders, we were asked to lead others into the surrounding village to preach. On the first day, I struggled to reach the Muslims. That night I asked God to help me because I did not know what to do.

He said to me: "You have more in common with the Muslims than you think . . . Abraham is your starting place."

I know a lot about Abraham, the Father of Faith. He had a covenant with God. He was to be a father of many Nations. He was promised his descendants would be numbered like the innumerable stars in Heaven or like the sands on the seashore.

Kings would come out from Him and nations would be affected. God promised that through His seed, all the nations of the Earth would be blessed through this promise.

The Muslims believe in Abraham. So the next day, armed with a fresh revelation from God, I talked to the Muslims about Abraham, repeating to them all the things I know about the promised blessings to all families on the Earth.

Many had family members who were sick. I asked them if these sicknesses were a blessing or a curse. They agreed that the sicknesses were not a blessing. I shared with them that I had discovered how to receive the blessing of Abraham. I shared that as a Christian, I have discovered that the secret to receiving the blessing of Abraham was through Jesus Christ. I told them that I could prove it and if they allowed me to pray for their sick, I would impart the blessing of Abraham to them. If I were right, the sicknesses they had would immediately leave their bodies. With their permission, I laid hands upon their sick. I said, "I impart the blessing of Abraham into your body in the name of Jesus Christ!" I prayed in tongues until I knew that God had delivered them from the curse of sickness.

You know what happened next? All of them were healed within minutes.

> For as many as are of the works of the law are under the curse; for it is written: Cursed is every one that continueth not in all things which are written in the book of the law to do them. (Galatians 3:10)

> Christ hath redeemed us from the curse of the law, being made a curse for us; for it is written: Cursed *is* every one that hangeth on a tree: *That the blessing of Abraham might come on the Gentiles through Jesus Christ; that we might receive the promise of the Spirit through faith.* (Galatians 3:13–14, italics mine)

There is tremendous power in preaching the cross of Christ. As He hung on that cross, the law of carnal commandments was nailed to it, taking them out of our way. Every curse of the law was removed. This deliverance through the cross restores all who will believe to wholeness. The blessing of Abraham comes by faith in Jesus Christ.

As the revelation became more real to me, I could tell people with confidence that they would be free from the curse of sickness. What a wonderful time it was to watch as the blessing of Abraham came into the lives of these Muslim families. Abraham's blessing is truly unchangeable. Christ redeemed us from the entire curse of the law. We are Abraham's seed in Christ Jesus. When we have faith in the finished work of Christ and realize that we are free from dead works (keeping the law), the curse ends in Christ. Jesus is *the year of Jubilee*; all debts have been cancelled through Him. *Praise God forever!*

The redemption offered to every family of the Earth is powerful. God's promise to Abraham through Jesus Christ is an everlasting one. He meant it. It was guaranteed and sealed in the broken body and the blood of Jesus Christ. It is, strikingly, as powerful today as it was the day He made the promise to Abraham. God is still honoring His promise to Abraham. To have faith is to believe that what God said **HE** would do, **HE** is able to perform.

What an amazing revelation I received that day. The revelation of Christ released the keys of the kingdom to Peter. The key to healing the Muslims was placed into my hands. Kingdom keys carry great power; the revelation of Jesus brings them into your hand. Every Muslim prayed for during the entire trip was instantly healed because that promise is as good today as when God spoke it to Abraham.

God's power never diminishes over time. It is available 24 hours a day, 7 days a week. There are never any brownouts. No power shortages exist in God.

Praise his wonderful name.
He is so generous.
His loving kindness endures forever.
He is always faithful to his word.

When we believe His word and take Him at His word, miracles are suddenly at hand. His kingdom **is** at hand. *If you don't believe this, repent and believe the gospel.*

This is what it is like to be at rest—living in the power of a resurrected life—having full confidence in the finished work of Jesus Christ; free from slavery. Communion should bring us back to the state of *it is finished*—a state of rest, of peace and harmony with the One who sits on the throne. Don't try to keep the law; it is bad for your health. It can kill you before your time.

5

RECALLING CHRIST

Say not in thine heart: Who shall ascend into
Heaven? (that is, to bring Christ down from
above). Or: Who shall descend into the deep?
(that is, to bring Christ up again from the dead).
(Romans 10:6–7)

Recalling Christ—thinking there is something more He
must do—is evidence of not understanding what was
done in His body. The above Scripture suggests that certain
beliefs constitute a false attempt to either try to raise Him again
or to bring Him down from above.

Misunderstanding His body causes such futile exercises to
occur. When we approach God in error, we make a case for His
mercy; but our lack in approaching Him according to Scripture
is why so many people are sick, weak, and why some sleep.

Needless suffering and premature death are part of this
problem. When Christ finished His work here on Earth, there
was no need for Him to come do anything again, including
healing anyone, because He already did it all. It was finished
when He said it was, and it was perfect. As His body, we are

to deliver to each other His finished work in both word and deed. This means that because of His finished work and our subsequent acceptance of the King, His kingdom has come to abide in *us*—His body—and we have the word of faith in us to command or to take charge of impossible situations, bringing the remedy required in the moment. There is no need to ask Jesus to come and do for us what He has already delegated us to do in His name.

> For Moses describeth the righteousness which is of the law; that the man which doeth those things shall live by them. But the righteousness, which is of faith, speaketh on this wise. Say not in thine heart: Who shall ascend into Heaven? (that is, to bring Christ down from above); or: Who shall descend into the deep? (that is, to bring up Christ again from the dead). But what saith it? The word is nigh thee, even in thy mouth, and in thy heart; that is, the word of faith, which we preach: That if thou shalt confess with thy mouth the Lord Jesus, and shalt believe in thine heart that God hath raised Him from the dead, thou shalt be saved.
>
> For with the heart, man believeth unto righteousness; and with the mouth, confession is made unto salvation. For the Scripture saith: Whosoever believeth on him shall not be ashamed. For there is no difference between the Jew and the Greek; for the same Lord over all is rich unto all that call upon him. For whosoever shall call upon the name of the Lord, shall be saved. (Romans 10:5–13)

The realization that there is nothing more to achieve outside of the finished work of Christ, frees us from the works of the law and transports us into righteousness, which is by faith.

Faith becomes what we now speak because we believe in His finished work.

But speaking is only the beginning of believing. Speaking is not sufficient evidence of belief. A man that speaks but lacks action is disconnected from reality. He has a claim to faith by words, but without actions that prove his stated convictions, there is no tangible evidence to his claims. Belief is not the same thing as thought. Thought is a mental exercise and can be done independently of action.

When Jesus walked the Earth as a Jewish man, He spoke Aramaic. Our Old Testament is in the Hebrew language. The word for "hear," which is *shema* (pronounced schma) has a double meaning: *to hear; to obey.*

The English language defines hearing as a function of sound waves and vibrations within the auditory system monitoring sound. Discernible sounds can be understood. The Western ear is satisfied with this definition, but the Jewish definition does not end with auditory function. Hearing to the Jew is fully understood when he has obeyed what was discerned through hearing. *Shema* means *to hear, to obey.* To hear the word of God is not *shema* unless you are obedient to *perform* what you have heard God say.

Your mother tells you to do something. Yes . . . you heard her, but is the task completed? If not, in her mind, you didn't hear her. If you did hear, then the task would now be finished or at the very least, in process.

"I thought I told you to wash the car; didn't you hear me?"

"Of course I heard you."

"Then why is the car still dirty?"

The evidence of hearing is in the obedient performance of the command. Have you done what you heard? If not, you have not heard what you were instructed to do in the sense of shema. *The evidence of hearing to the Jew is the response of obedience.*

Jesus says, "He that has ears to hear, let him hear." In the English language, we interpret His statement to mean *if you have ears attached to your head, you should use them.* But to the Jewish ear, this same statement means *he that has ears to hear (shema), let him obey (shema).* In Hebrew, hearing and obeying mean the same thing.

> Not everyone that saith unto me *Lord*, shall enter into the Kingdom of Heaven; but he that *doeth the will of my Father* which is in Heaven shall enter. Many will say to me in that day, Lord, Lord, have we not prophesied in thy name? And in thy name have cast out devils? And in thy name done many wonderful works? And then will I profess unto them: I never knew you; depart from me, ye that work iniquity. (Matthew 7:21–23, italics mine)

Shema is wisdom. *Doing the will of God . . .* this is what is recognized in the Kingdom of Heaven. Hearing God without applying obedience is not hearing Him. Hearing and putting into action what He instructs separates the wise from the foolish, the obedient from the disobedient.

> Therefore, whosoever *heareth* these sayings of mine and *doeth* them, I will liken him unto a wise man, which built his house upon a rock. And the rain descended, and the floods came, and the winds blew, and beat upon that house; and it fell not, for it was founded upon a rock. And every one that heareth these sayings of mine, and doeth them not, shall be likened unto a foolish man, which built his house upon the sand. And the rain descended, and the floods came, and the winds blew, and beat upon that house; and it fell—and great was the fall of it. (Matthew 7:24–27)

The foundational rock is evident in the doing,
not in the hearing alone.

Hearing God without obedience may fit into an English dictionary, but not into a Hebrew one. Transformation comes when hearing and obeying God become reality and not theory—not just head knowledge, but obedient action.

When we become transformed by the renewing of our minds, we are able to prove what the will of God is. Hearing the will of God is only complete when you *do* the will of God.

> I beseech you therefore, brethren, by the mercies of God, that ye present your bodies a living sacrifice; holy, acceptable unto God, which is your reasonable service. Be not conformed to this world but be ye transformed by the renewing of your mind that ye might *prove* what is the good, acceptable and perfect will of God. (Romans 12:1–2)

Re-calling Jesus to do something for you that He has already done is unbelief. Remembering what God has done through the broken body of Christ gives us the substance of faith. We speak what was written and also performed by Christ. Through His broken body, we have been given access by faith to all things, including body parts. The word, when spoken in faith, honors the present truth. The present truth describes what we now have in Christ because of what He did.

Who we are in Christ is because of what He did, and
the authority and ministry we have been called to is be-
cause of what He did.

Jesus did what He did to empower a new creation to oper-
ate as sons of God in the Earth.

We now bear His name. We Have been called by His name to do the same works that He did and greater because He has gone to the Father and has sent the Holy Spirit *to train us in these present truths.*

A new heart for the man who's heart is physically damaged. A new pancreas to replace a defective one in the diabetic. A new liver for the alcoholic. There are men and women of God who believe these things were made possible through the broken body of Jesus, the children's bread that came down from Heaven. They declare it openly and take responsibility to enforce this reality in those around them, in both word and deed.

Unfortunately, false doctrine has constrained the body's ability to believe what Christ has already accomplished. God has called us to be transformed by the renewing of our minds and has delegated us to prove what His will is. His will is that His kingdom be fully activated in the church at large—that His church accepts responsibility for its calling to bring the kingdom everywhere the soles of its feet go.

When we are free to believe the impossible because of what Christ has done, our speaking changes to the kind of righteousness that is by faith; *and we speak great things*—things that get the attention of Heaven, things that activate the blessings of the finished work of Christ into His body, the church. People so affected begin to *act in the place of the risen Christ* and perform miracles that stagger the imagination. The same Spirit of faith released in the resurrection, reaches into the mind of Christ and operates in the authority Jesus empowered His disciples with.

> Then he called his twelve disciples together, and gave them power and authority over all devils, and to cure diseases. And he sent them to preach the Kingdom of God, and to heal the sick. (Luke 9:1–2)

Jesus gave to His disciples authority over all devils and to cure diseases. He then sent them out to preach the Kingdom of God and to heal the sick. They heard him, but what they heard was activated by obedience as they went out and preached and healed the sick. What good is authority, if you don't use it?

Transformation occurs when we go out obeying His directions and by becoming healers. A healer has been given authority to heal, so he obeys the commands by going out to preach the kingdom and to heal. The evidence is real. The healings took place. The devils were subject unto them.

The disciples observed Jesus healing others, but now were directed to become the healers themselves and were given the authority to do so. So it is with us.

Again He sent out seventy, giving them instructions concerning their journey. They, too, went out as the disciples had before. They were so excited upon their return and reported their experience.

> The seventy returned again with joy, saying, "Lord, even the devils are subject unto us through thy name." (Luke 10:17)

He realigned the focus of the disciples as they reported their victories while released under His mandate. When they thrilled themselves with the noticeable authority, and how the devils were subject unto them, He told them to rejoice instead that their names were written in the Book of Life. By so doing, they would operate more closely within the mandate of loving one another, rather than the thrill of the power vested in them. Loving others was to be their focus because faith works by love.

> He said unto them, "I beheld Satan as lightning fall from Heaven. Behold, I give unto you power to tread on serpents and scorpions, and over all the power of the enemy, and nothing shall by any means hurt you. Notwithstanding in this

rejoice not, that the spirits are subject unto you;
but rather rejoice, because your names are written in Heaven." (Luke 10:18–20)

Those names written in Heaven are the sons of their Father.
God is love; His motivations are pure about those souls who
need to be converted.

We, too, have this same direction.

This is a Kingdom direction, not a worldly direction. The
command comes from His Kingdom; when obeyed, the command carries Kingdom authority to whoever will hear it and
obey it.

The proof of obedience is healed people.
Healed people are evidence of a mind having gone through
kingdom transformation.

Jesus drove this point home to me very clearly one day. I will
never forget the lesson, for it has etched my heart permanently.

A friend of mine had died. While driving home from
Calgary, Alberta to Red Deer, she was on my heart. My first
instinct is to go and raise a person from the dead—this is just
what you do as far as I am concerned. So during the drive
home, I was imagining myself raising her from the dead. All
the way home, I was thanking God for His word and quoting
Scriptures about the dead being raised. Going over and over
them, stirring myself up by way of pure remembrance and
declaring a successful outcome.

I did this for the better part of an hour and a half. When I
got home, I walked through the door and kept right on preaching on raising the dead. My two roommates were there and an
aboriginal man and woman. When they heard me say that I

was going to raise the dead, the man said, "You can't raise the dead. Only God can raise the dead!"

I said, "I beg your pardon; Jesus said that those who believe on Him will do the works He did; if He raised the dead, then so will I! I will heal the sick, cast out devils, raise the dead and cleanse lepers."

After a few more minutes of preaching this way, the aboriginal woman asked, "Frank, do you mean to tell me that *you* can heal me?"

I said, "Absolutely. Stand on your feet and I will prove it."

She looked very shocked and said, "You can't be serious."

I said to her, "You won't know unless you stand up, will you? Do you want to be healed or don't you?"

"Yes," she said.

"So stand to your feet," I replied. I anointed her with oil in the name of Jesus, and immediately she felt warmth, which began at her head and permeated her whole body, healing her completely of an upper back problem that had caused years of chronic pain.

You need to realize that this was done while I was filled with the Holy Ghost. Being in the Spirit and performing what is written is different than just doing acts for the purpose of lording it over the devil in a sense of pride. A mind transformed has its affections set on Heaven and a desire to do things as God directs. That's why a transformed mind presents its body and all that this implies toward hearing and obeying. I want to hear today. A transformed mind realizes that Jesus has a current ministry as Lord.

A transformed mind has the *ability to prove* the will of God. Why? *Because it is loyal to the voice of God and is obedient to perform what is commanded.* A mind conformed to the world cannot prove anything because it has not taken responsibility to perform commands. *Believing is evidenced by action—not words alone.*

When you hear and do, that is when you have built your house upon a rock. *Hearing without doing is deception.*

THE PERFECT LAW OF LIBERTY

> Wherefore lay apart all filthiness and superfluity of naughtiness, and receive with meekness the engrafted word, which is able to save your souls. But be ye doers of the word, and not hearers only, deceiving your own selves. For if any be a hearer of the word, and not a doer, he is like unto a man beholding his natural face in a glass; for he beholdeth himself, and goeth his way, and straightway forgetteth what manner of man he was. But who so looketh into the perfect law of liberty, and continueth therein, he being not a forgetful hearer, but a doer of the work; this man shall be blessed in his deed. (James 1:21–25)

James is describing the process of being blessed. It is a transforming process beginning with laying apart all filthiness and superfluity of naughtiness. Forsaking all and in meekness receiving the engrafted word.

The engrafted word of God finds a home in your soul, delivering your soul.

Unless you obey what you are receiving (the engrafted word), you stay in bondage to self-deception. Am I called to heal the sick? Yes, because Jesus said it. The engrafted word would be finding the will of God through studying to show myself approved unto God. But if the approval of God *is evidenced* when I heal a sick person, then the only way not to be deceived is *to find sick people and pray for them*. Without doing the works, I have not obeyed His will. This is an example of a house built upon the sand.

The Perfect law of liberty—doing on a regular basis what has been commanded—causes me to become seasoned in my obedience, competent in application of His word, and able to teach others—not in word only but also by example.

Am I a man of obedience? If so, I am a man of action. A man of action does what he is commanded to do. He is free from any voices that would confront his authority and his actions do not depend on anything but hearing and doing. No one can take away from him what God has given.

> Behold, I come quickly; hold that fast which
> thou hast, that no man take thy crown. (Reve-
> lation 3:11)

Eventually, the gainsayers are silenced because the man of obedience makes full proof of the calling in spite of his critics. He isn't going to let any man take the crown of authority that Jesus has given him. Jesus modeled this behavior for us.

Jesus walked in the perfect law of liberty. The religious leaders of His day challenged Him on His authority. He was doing works. They wanted to know who had given Him authority to publicly behave the way He was behaving. Jesus never stopped doing His works because religious leaders frowned upon them. He kept right on going and doing what was in His heart. He was not intimidated, they were. He was about His Father's business. *Allowing man to dictate to Him what He could and could not do was not part of His thought process.* He did not fear man. He was only interested in doing what His Father asked of Him. Jesus operated under the law of liberty, doing what God commanded. His approval came not from man, but from God.

> Ye men of Israel, hear these words: Jesus of
> Nazareth, *a man approved of God* among you by

miracles and wonders and signs, which God did
by him in the midst of you, as ye yourselves also
know. (Acts 2:22, italics mine)

Jesus was approved of God among those in Jerusalem (Peter's
audience in this sermon). Peter is pointing to the miracles, wonders and signs *as the evidence* of God's approval. The works that
God did through him, *as ye yourselves also know*. His obedience
to the work God gave him, the actions he took, and the signs that
followed, were the evidence of the approval of God.

What is the evidence of God's approval in you? Are you
studying with a resolve to obey what He says to you? *Miracles,
signs and wonders are the evidence of such a reality.* The law of
liberty is clear: *freedom is doing the will of God*. When we do
the will of God, signs follow us. Those not doing the will of
God are threatened. They might have positions in the church.
They might think they are approved of God themselves, but
they lack the *evidence of obedience*.

Noah Webster (1828) defines "heresy" as

Heresy: n. [Gr. *from, to take, to hold.* ; L. *haersis*; Fr. *heresie*]

1. A fundamental error in religion or an error of opinion respecting some fundamental doctrine of religion.
   Because the Scriptures are the standard of faith, any
   opinion that is repugnant to its doctrines, is heresy.

2. Heresy, in law, is an offense against Christianity that
   consists of the denial of some of its essential doctrines,
   publicly avowed and obstinately maintained.

For there must be also heresies among you, *that
they which are approved,* may be made manifest
among you. (1 Corinthians 11:19)

Notice that Paul is contrasting heresy with approval. He is saying that heresy becomes obvious when contrasted *by the evidence of the approved ones.* Those approved of God are made manifest when heresy is present. Those approved of God get results, while those in error are exposed as having no fruit.

> And he came to Nazareth, where he had been brought up; and as his custom was, he went into the synagogue on the Sabbath day, and stood up to read. And there was delivered unto him the book of the prophet Esaias. And when he had opened the book, he found the place where it was written: The Spirit of the Lord *is* upon me, because he hath anointed me to preach the gospel to the poor; he hath sent me to heal the brokenhearted, to preach deliverance to the captives, and to recover sight to the blind, to set at liberty them that are bruised; to preach the acceptable year of the Lord. And he closed the book, and he gave *it* again to the minister, and sat down. And the eyes of all them that were in the synagogue were fastened on him. (Luke 4:16–20)

So far so good . . . speaking the word of God is what we do; it is our custom as it was in the day of Christ, nothing out of the ordinary—He sat down—the people were watching him.

> And he began to say unto them: This day is this Scripture fulfilled in your ears. And all bare him witness and wondered at the gracious words which proceeded out of his mouth. And they said: Is not this Joseph's son? And he said unto them: Ye will surely say unto me this proverb; Physician, heal thyself: whatsoever we have heard done in Capernaum, do also here in thy country. (Luke 4:21)

It began to sink in to those in attendance that Jesus had just accepted ownership of His mission with an announcement that these Scriptures were being fulfilled in their ears. *Jesus has claimed His prophetic identity in the hearing of the people.* He had stood up and given notice that He was the *approved one. He declared himself to be what God said He was, refusing to wear the label that the mob wanted to know him as "nothing special—just Joseph's son."*

He explained to them that although He would perform great miracles, wonders and signs among the people in Capernaum, He would be mocked on His next visit to Nazareth.

> And he said: Verily I say unto you, no prophet is accepted in his own country. But I tell you of a truth, many widows were in Israel in the days of Elias, when the Heaven was shut up three years and six months, when great famine was throughout all the land. But unto none of them was Elias sent, save unto Sarepta, a city of Sidon, unto a woman that was a widow. And many lepers were in Israel in the time of Eliseus the prophet, and none of them was cleansed, saving Naaman the Syrian. (Luke 4:24–27)

As Jesus continues, He gives examples of two historical people familiar to all, who when they heard the prophetic word, responded in faith and obedience to the word given. In so doing, they received miracles, wonders and signs. However, the mob failed to *see Jesus through the words of the prophets,* but through unbelieving eyes. *When He called them on their heresy, they attempted to kill Him.*

Imagine going from being admired and having goodwill among those who know you, to being the object of a murderous mob within ten minutes.

Yet this continues to happen whenever a person stands up and *claims their prophetic identity in Christ Jesus* and takes ownership of the responsibility to be a doer of the word of God.

Is it unfathomable that when a believer discovers it is possible to do what Jesus says he can do, that he stakes his claim upon the word of God, accessing and activating divine graces? Why does this make people so angry? Why is there a mob ready to beat down believers who stand up? Why is it so uncommon for one to believe he can do what Christ said that he can? Jesus made His claim right in the synagogue. I like what my friend Gary Hicks used to say, "Throw a rock into a pack of dogs and you need not ask which one you hit." Well, Jesus didn't need to ask which ones were insulted by His claim; *they all wanted to kill Him.*

When you stand up, boldly declaring that you heal the sick, people may throw you a strange look, but that may be because it is rare. If, instead, they embrace the *prophetic testimony*, they will be healed, like my native friend was healed *when she stood up*, willing to follow a prophetic command (*stand up*) that led to her healing.

Any opinion that is doctrinally incorrect opposes the purposes of God and is heresy. Paul said that this heresy causes those who are approved of God to be manifested in our midst. *Praise the Lord.*

We are contending for the faith that was once delivered to the saints. Many are breaking through the veils of heresy and claiming their prophetic destiny like Jesus did in His hometown. Stand up today in your hometown and let others know that you are the one to call when they need a miracle, because you have faith in God. Let them know that the words of Jesus concerning your prophetic destiny to do His works are fulfilled in their ears this day. Take those who believe with you, and go empty a hospital in His name. *You can do it!*

Jesus has a present ministry being

- Lord
- Surety
- Great high priest
- Mediator
- Advocate
- Intercessor

When we study to show ourselves approved of God, we realize that while we can do the works of Christ, we do not work alone, nor is the work exclusive to ourselves. Jesus need not come back and do what He did during His earthly ministry for us. It is finished. But His continuing ministry facilitates and empowers all that we do. His work as the *great high priest*, a priest forever after the order of Melchizedek, is still a functional and eternal ministry.

When we approach the Father through Him, He mediates and advocates for us as the head of the body and as Lord. When we approach God by faith, according to what was accomplished by Christ during His earthly ministry, Christ as the head of the body is mediating and watching over the word concerning all things. He is interceding for us. The One who is perfect in every detail of the new covenant is presiding over it and interceding for you. He is advocating your petitions, brought to your Father.

When we rightly discern the Lord's body, we will approach the Father based upon what Jesus' broken body and blood have already done for us. We will approach Him in *the present truth*—reality lived in truth through what He did on the cross, in the grave, in the resurrection, and in His ascension to the place of His continuing ministry.

> Wherefore I will not be negligent to put you
> always in remembrance of these things, though
> ye know them, and be established in the present
> truth. (2 Peter 1:12)

When we approach God in present truth, we realize that what Jesus did for us is *presently real* and *eternally powerful*. We are not asking Him to do it again, but we are standing in faith in the finished work of Christ during His earthly ministry and in light of the present truth. *He presides over the present truth. Both His ministry on Earth and His present ministry created the present realities of the inheritance of sons.* He presides over this present reality and advocates for us on our behalf.

We take our stand against sickness. Through the power we have been given over all the power of the enemy, we boldly stand *in the confidence of surety*, who it was that did what was needed to give us the victory. Because He lives, we can count on all of Heaven's resources and all power in Heaven and Earth to be immediately at our disposal. This is present reality in present truth.

> By so much was Jesus made a *surety* of a better
> testament. And they truly were many priests,
> because they were not suffered to continue by
> reason of death: But this man, because he con-
> tinueth ever, hath an unchangeable priesthood.
> Wherefore he is able also to save them to the
> uttermost that come unto God by him, seeing
> he ever liveth to make intercession for them.
> (Hebrews 7:22–25, italics mine)

Noah Webster (1828) gives us this meaning of "suretyship":

Suretyship: n. [from *surety*] The state of being surety; *the obligation of a person to answer for another*, and make good any debt or loss which may occur from another's delinquency.

> And whatsoever ye shall ask in my name, that
> will I do, that the Father may be glorified in the
> Son. (John 14:13)

The Scripture preceding John 14:13 says this:

> Verily, verily I say unto you: He that believeth
> on me, the works that I do shall he do also; and,
> greater works than these shall he do; because I
> go unto my Father. (John 14:12)

He has become surety, obligating Himself to answer for another. If I am doing His works, I can ask the Father whatever I will, and Jesus will do it so that the Father may be glorified. Jesus is the great high priest of our profession, our advocate with the Father, a mediator of the new covenant. He stands *in the present reality* of His eternal priesthood presiding over the finished work: the blood on the mercy seat testifies that it is finished; the veil, His flesh, testifies that the new and living way is opened. The resulting present truth that we are becoming established in is guaranteed through the surety (Jesus, the mediator between God and man) presiding over it.

It gives me hope to believe that when I come to my Father, established in the present truth, Jesus is mediating on my behalf as my advocate with the Father and as a surety of any delinquency on my part. As my personal intercessor, I have faith to believe that He will pray for me to remember His death and what it did for me and for you. He is forever faithful, forever true. I can count on Him. My trust is in Him.

What a wonderful savior. He is able to save to the uttermost. Until you take your last breath, His faithfulness will be your comfort in this life. The more you acknowledge Him, the greater His influence will be in your daily guidance.

You are connected to Him.
He is the true vine and we are His branches.
He has the words of life.
Life has no other source,
He is eternal life.

6

BODY OF HIS FLESH

Both Jew and Gentile are now reconciled into one body. The enmity between Jew and Gentile was slain in that one body on the cross. All nations now have access to a great salvation. *What a wonderful Lord.*

> Having abolished in his flesh the enmity, even the law of commandments contained in ordinances; for to make *in himself of twain one new man*, so making peace; And that he might reconcile both unto God in one body by the cross, having slain the enmity thereby. (Ephesians 2:15–16, italics mine)

> And he is the head of the body, the church: who is the beginning, the firstborn from the dead; that in all *things* he might have the preeminence. For it pleased *the Father* that in him should all fullness dwell; And, **having made peace** <u>through the blood of his cross</u>, by him to reconcile all things unto himself; by him, *I*

say, whether *they be* things in Earth, or things in Heaven. (Colossians 1:18–20)

This is our reassurance that the blood of His cross has reconciled everything in Heaven and Earth. *He has reconciled all things unto himself.*

7

THE BODY OF SIN

> For the law having a shadow of good things to come, and not the very image of the things, can never with those sacrifices which they offered year by year continually make the comers thereunto perfect. For then would they not have ceased to be offered? Because that the worshippers once purged should have had no more conscience of sins. (Hebrews 10:1–2)

This Scripture refers to the sacrifices made under the law, which had a shadow of good things to come, and not the very image of things. This meant the sacrifices were pointing to something that would be perfect, but yet was not perfect as they were offered under the old way. *They lacked completeness; wholeness, perfection.* They could not make those offering sacrifices **perfect**.

Consider Noah Webster's 1828 definition of the word "perfect":

Perfect: [L. *perfectus, perficio,* to complete; *per* and *facio,* to do or make through; to carry to the end]

Finished; complete; consummate; not defective; having all that is requisite to its nature and kind.

1. To finish or complete as to leave nothing wanting

   a. "If we love one another, God dwelleth in us and his love is perfected in us." (1 John 4)

Once the worshippers were purged, they should have had no more consciousness of sin. Notice that their sacrifices were worship. In their worship, there was a remembrance of something done every year: the remembrance of their sins. Remembering their sin continually reminded them that they were not yet made perfect.

Imagine living your entire life remembering your sins as worship; the consciousness of sin as your continual reminder. Imagine a reminder of the evil within your heart every year while your heart condemns you. Every year you make that sacrifice, never coming to perfection, always deficient, never measuring up to the impossible standards of the law. Do you still worship under the old model, condemning yourself, *re-member-ing* your sins as you try to be *good*? For the Old Testament worshippers, these were *dead* works. But they did point to something coming that would make them perfect.

> But in those sacrifices there is a remembrance again made of sins every year. For it is not possible that the blood of bulls and of goats should take away sins. Wherefore when he cometh into the world, he saith, Sacrifice and offering thou wouldest not, but a body hast thou prepared me: In burnt offerings and sacrifices for sin thou hast had no pleasure. Then said I, Lo, I come (in the volume of the book it is written

of me,) to do thy will, O God. Above when he
said, Sacrifice and offering and burnt offerings
and offering for sin thou wouldest not, neither
hadst pleasure therein; which are offered by
the law; Then said he, Lo, I come to do thy will,
O God. He taketh away the first, that he may
establish the second. (Hebrews 10:3–9)

Thank God He took away that first imperfect shadow of
worship, where the people were unable to have their sins taken
away, that He may establish the second. Would the second act
of worship really take away the sins of the people? Would this
body that He prepared, when sacrificed, be able to make the
people perfect? The first act of worship had no remedy for taking away sins or for the conscience: **worshippers once purged
should have had no more conscience of sins** (Hebrews 10:2).
This perfection had to eliminate sin from the conscience.

By the which will we are sanctified through the
offering of the body of Jesus Christ once for all.
And every priest standeth daily ministering and
offering oftentimes the same sacrifices, which
can never take away sins: But this man, after
he had offered one sacrifice for sins forever, sat
down on the right hand of God; From hence-
forth expecting till his enemies be made his
footstool. (Hebrews 10:10–13)

This is the covenant that I will make with them
after those days, saith the Lord, I will put my
laws into their hearts, and in their minds will I
write them; And their sins and iniquities will I
remember no more. (Hebrews 10:16–17)

He is not remembering your sins anymore because they
have been taken away—through one sacrifice made once and
for all—for everybody.

> Now where remission of these is, there is no more offering for sin. Having therefore, brethren, boldness to enter into the holiest by the blood of Jesus, by a new and living way, which he hath consecrated for us, through the veil, that is to say, his flesh; And having an high priest over the house of God; Let us draw near with a true heart in full assurance of faith, having our hearts sprinkled from an evil conscience, and our bodies washed with pure water. (Hebrews 10:18–22)

Once He finished being the sacrifice, died, and was resurrected, He was resurrected to hold a new position in Heaven. He is now **the High Priest over the house of God** (Hebrews 10:21). From this priesthood, He accepts those who draw near with a true heart, and in full assurance of faith, those hearts are sprinkled from an evil conscience. Their bodies are washed with pure water.

FORGETTING SIN

*One day, two days . . . 15 days. Wait a minute, how could I forget to sin? Gee, it's been 15 days since I did that thing that I do. How could I have gone 15 days without remembering to do **that**? Usually I can't stop thinking about my sin. It's as if I forgot about the rules and strategies I was using to combat my sin for the past 15 days. What happened? What is happening to me? I feel free not only from sin but from the strategies I use to fight against sin as well.*

> Know ye not, brethren, (for I speak to them that
> know the law,) how that the law hath dominion
> over a man as long as he liveth? (Romans 7:1)

Paul is speaking *to them that know the law*. Under the law, the woman is bound by the law of her husband. Whatever the husband says is her law, but if her husband dies, she is free from the law of her husband.

> For the woman which hath an husband is bound
> by the law to *her* husband so long as he liveth;
> but if the husband be dead, she is loosed from
> the law of *her* husband. (Romans 7:2)

In the book of Romans, chapter seven is a pivotal key to understanding your freedom from the law. What you should know is that God himself was the husband Paul is speaking about.

> For thy Maker is thine husband; the LORD of
> hosts is his name; and thy Redeemer the Holy
> One of Israel; The God of the whole Earth shall
> he be called. (Isaiah 54:5)

The only way those under the law could ever be free from the law of their husband would be if the husband (God) were to die.

> So then if, while her husband liveth, she be
> married to another man, she shall be called
> an adulteress: but if her husband be dead, she
> is free from that law; so that she is no adulter-
> ess, though she be married to another man.
> (Romans 7:3)

Jesus was the body prepared for God to come down and die in. God had never died before, having no beginning and no end in eternity. He had to present himself in the body of a man.

It was in this body that He became obedient to the will of God all the way to death, even the death of the cross. And so, here is the husband of those under His law, coming in a body prepared to be a sacrifice and dying.

His death frees His wife to be the wife of another. Her former husband, now dead, no longer has any claim to her or rule over her. The law, concerning the carnal commandment is now taken away and nailed to the cross that her husband hung on, symbolizing her complete freedom from His law.

Now she is free to marry another. The law of her new husband, the firstborn from the dead, is as powerful as the law of her former husband, but with one exception: there is no curse associated with the new law. It simply states that now "**ye love one another**"; this is to fulfill the law of your new husband.

But Paul also said that the law has dominion over a man as long as he lives. This means that the husband died, but because I am alive, I am not free from the law.

> Knowing this, that our old man is crucified with him, that the body of sin might be destroyed, that henceforth we should not serve sin. (Romans 6:6)

God's answer to your dilemma was for you to die also, to be crucified with Christ, dying with Him. The old man dies in Christ, and the body of sin destroyed with the enmity between God and man being slain in that single act. Out of that death, another birth came forth. Jesus rose from the dead as the firstborn of every creature. He is the new husband of the new creation. Now you, who were raised with Him when He resurrected from the dead, have a new law. Your new husband has declared that His law of the Spirit of life frees you from the law of sin and death.

A new man emerges, free from the law the old man had to keep. The old man has been declared dead and buried in the waters of baptism. The new man is free from keeping the law.

> What shall we say then? Is the law sin? God for-
> bid. Nay, I had not known sin, but by the law:
> for I had not known lust, except the law had
> said, Thou shalt not covet. But sin, taking occa-
> sion by the commandment, wrought in me all
> manner of concupiscence. For without the law
> sin was dead. For I was alive without the law
> once: but when the commandment came, sin
> revived, and I died. (Romans 7:7–9)

Sin is dead. The commandments of the first husband are gone. If I focus on the commandments of the former husband, it gives sin an occasion to begin working in me. Where there is no commandment, there is no sin. The knowledge of sin came through the law. If the law is no longer in force because the husband who brought the law is dead, then I am free from the law. Sin has lost its power. Sin shall not have dominion over me because; now I am married to a new husband. My new husband's law is simple: *love one another*.

If I don't understand this, I will remain under the power of sin. But when I realize that I cannot be condemned under the law of a dead husband, I cannot be called an adulterer; nor am I required to remember the old life, with the old rules and the old consequences (death). I already died. I can't die twice.

A Miracle—Dealing with the Conscience

David was a man after God's heart. As he looked into the worship in the old covenant, he saw something: a revelation that had to do with *Hyssop*; the Hebrew word is *Ezov*.

In the Old Testament, the Israelites enslaved in Egypt used Ezov in the Passover ritual. They used it to sprinkle lamb's blood on the door posts and lintels of the slaves' quarters so that the Lord would pass over them as he slew the firstborn of the Egyptians. Once the Israelites were in the wilderness, and later, when they had settled in Israel, they used Ezov regularly for other rituals, such as the ritual for cleansing from leprosy and for ritual purification. In Psalms, the sprinkling of Ezov is used allegorically to refer to purification of the heart.

> Behold, I was shapen in iniquity; and in sin did my mother conceive me. Behold, thou desirest truth in the inward parts: and in the hidden part thou shalt make me to know wisdom. Purge me with hyssop, and I shall be clean: wash me, and I shall be whiter than snow. Make me to hear joy and gladness; that the bones which thou hast broken may rejoice. Hide thy face from my sins, and blot out all mine iniquities. (Psalm 51:5–9)

David was asking God to "*purge me with Hyssop, and I shall be clean: wash me and I shall be whiter than snow.*" He wanted to be clean; his conscience was very disturbed about killing a man so he could take that man's wife. *He saw how hyssop was used to sprinkle blood upon the altar as a cleansing ritual.* David was saying: *cleanse me; wash me, I want to be clean. I want your mercy—blot out all my iniquities.*

Under the old pattern, the sprinkling of blood could not cleanse the heart from an evil conscience. But after the priesthood changed, the New High Priest—Jesus Christ over the house of God—can sprinkle your heart from an evil conscience, cleansing it to take away guilt, condemnation and shame.

Isaiah foretold the fulfillment of a time when God Himself would cleanse us from our sins.

> Come now, and let us reason together, saith the LORD: though your sins be as scarlet, they shall be as white as snow; though they be red like crimson, they shall be as wool. (Isaiah 1:18)

> I, even I, am he that blotteth out thy transgressions for mine own sake, and will not remember thy sins. (Isaiah 43:25)

Jesus entered into the Holy of Holies in Heaven and put His blood on the mercy seat.

> Neither by the blood of goats and calves, but by his own blood he entered in once into the holy place, having obtained eternal redemption for us. (Hebrews 9:12)

> Now when these things were thus ordained, the priests went always into the first tabernacle, accomplishing the service of God. But into the second went the high priest alone once every year, not without blood, which he offered for himself, and for the errors of the people: The Holy Ghost this signifying, that the way into the holiest of all was not yet made manifest, while as the first tabernacle was yet standing. (Hebrews 9:6–8)

Jesus' entrance into the holy place was significant because the way into the holiest was finally consummated. This now means everyone may enter the holiest of all, through a new and living way.

His body of sin, a body slain, a body which had become a curse for us, is now giving us access through the veil (His flesh). The finished work of Jesus as a Lamb slain was complete as He sprinkled His holy blood on the heavenly mercy seat, satisfying the demands of justice under the law. When you realize that you have access into the place where you have been declared entirely holy by the blood of Jesus, there need be no more remembrance of sins.

> For he hath made him to be sin for us, who
> knew no sin; that we might be made the righ-
> teousness of God in him. (2 Corinthians 5:21)

This Body that God prepared as a sacrifice for all, once and for all, took away anything that would block our access. The High priest was the only one who once had access into the holiest place, but through Jesus, the veil was ripped from top to bottom.

> And not as Moses, which put a veil over his face,
> that the children of Israel could not stedfastly
> look to the end of that which is abolished: but
> their minds were blinded: for until this day
> remaineth the same veil untaken away in the
> reading of the old testament; which veil is done
> away in Christ. (2 Corinthians 3:13–14)

When we are in Christ, the veil that inhibited the children of Israel from seeing the finished work of the cross is removed. Because of this, we can read the Old Testament with the realization that *anything forbidding us from coming into the presence of God is now removed by the offering of Christ.* Now we are able to *steadfastly look* as we enter that holiest of all, with the identical righteousness and standing that Jesus has.

Now we can enter boldly. We are sons and daughters to righteousness, not slaves to sin. We are not descendants of sinful men (a son of man), but we have been born again and have become the *sinless sons and daughters* of God, in whom there is no sin. We are sinless sons and daughters born from the loins of a sinless God. There is no more offering for sin because there is no sin; it was taken away. Praise God!!

Slaves live in the servant quarters, but sons and daughters live in Daddy's house. We can approach Him with an open face, looking without breaking eye contact. We have no shame, we have no guilt; we have no need to look away. We have been sprinkled from an evil conscience, and our bodies have been washed in pure water.

This one-time only sacrifice did what the blood of bulls and goats could never do: it made the comers thereafter perfect because when sins were taken away; it made provision for the conscience. Our hearts are sprinkled from an evil conscience.

> Neither by the blood of goats and calves, but by his own blood he entered in once into the holy place, having obtained eternal redemption for us. For if the blood of bulls and of goats, and the ashes of an heifer sprinkling the unclean, sanctifieth to the purifying of the flesh: how much more shall the blood of Christ, who through the eternal Spirit offered himself without spot to God, purge your conscience from dead works to serve the living God? (Hebrews 9:12–14)

Your conscience now purged from dead works is able to serve the living God. Your conscience is not only clean, but free. The law could not do that, but in Christ it *is* done.

When Satan comes to lie to us, he attempts to get us to believe that nothing was done at the cross that frees us from sin. He attempts to put the veil back over our eyes, by convincing us to **remember our sins**. This is dead work. This was the worship of slaves under the law. Convincing us to remember sin is his attempt to get us to agree with keeping the law. This is when sin takes advantage of us through the old commandments of a dead husband. We then approach the Old Testament with a veil over our eyes, unable to see that we have no sin. Somehow, we feel obligated to remember sin instead of remembering that Jesus' body removed sin, taking it completely away.

Not only was sin removed, but keeping any part of the law was also removed. Satan tricks us into believing there is something very wrong with us, and we are lured into attempting to become perfect through the old worship of remembering sins.

But our worship is worshiping God in Spirit and in truth, not in remembering sin.

We are free from any of the requirements of the law. Satan tempts us to keep even one small part. He uses the law to veil our eyes from the power of the cross. The *entire law* is done away with in Christ.

The only commandment under Son-ship is that we believe on the lord Jesus Christ and that we love one another. When we do this, there is no more remembrance of sins. Our hearts are washed from an evil conscience.

> *We were crucified with him.* Knowing this, that our old man is crucified with him, that the body of sin might be destroyed, that henceforth we should not serve sin. (Romans 6:6)

The body of sin was destroyed. We should not serve sin. We have been freed from sin. What happens then when we sin?

> My little children, these things write I unto you, that ye sin not. And if any man sin, we have an advocate with the Father, Jesus Christ the righteous: and he is the propitiation for our sins: and not for ours only, but also for the sins of the whole world. (1 John 2:1–2)

Jesus becomes our lawyer, who presents our case before the Father. When we sin, fellowship is broken, but we have Jesus advocating for us. So what is our part when we sin?

> If we confess our sins, he is faithful and just to forgive us our sins, and to cleanse us from all unrighteousness. (1 John 1:9)

We simply confess our sins, Jesus forgives us, and immediately we are cleansed from all unrighteousness; restored completely.

Wherefore he is able also to save them to the uttermost that come unto God by him, seeing he ever liveth to make intercession for them. (Hebrews 7:25)

He took care of our sins by taking them away, but His ministry does not end there. He continually works on our behalf, as mediator of the Covenant, great High Priest, advocate and intercessor. All of these roles He does on our behalf. He is able to save to the uttermost, because He has all our bases covered.

This is very comforting. He is still lovingly, looking out for you. He is ever faithful and ever true.

8

THE WHOLE FAMILY

For this cause I bow my knees unto the Father
of our Lord Jesus Christ, of whom the whole
family in Heaven and Earth is named. (Ephesians 3:14–15)

I am from the United States; I grew up there and later moved
to Canada, where I have lived for 22 years. I used to go
home to the States to visit relatives every couple of years for a
while, but over time, the visits became fewer and less frequent.
Each of my siblings has their own life. Like me, they have their
struggles, setbacks, celebrations, and victories.

Although they are family, time and distance has caused us
not to be as connected as before. My home is now where my
kids are. We have our own family unit, and everything that life
brings us, we share together, whether good or bad. As far as the
folks back home—out of sight, out of mind. Even though time
and distance separated us, all it took was one week at a family
reunion together to bring back our connections and make
them solid again.

My family in the States planned for the whole family to join for a reunion in Nashville, Tennessee during a convention my company was having at the Opryland Hotel. Since everyone was busy with their work lives, coordinating was very difficult. But, by some miracle, *the whole family showed up*, which is no small feat when you consider six siblings, their spouses, all the children, and Mom and Dad.

At the reunion, revisiting a funny childhood photo changed our hearts toward each other. When we were kids between the ages of two to six, we had a portrait taken of us all together. In the photo, we were in our play clothes. All of us were dirty. My sister's shirt was wet with drool, and a day before the picture was taken, I tried my hand at hairdressing. As a result, my sister had a two-inch section of her bangs missing. My sin was still there, captured for all time in a photo.

I decided to present to my siblings the bright idea to get dressed up just like we were in the photo; dirty our clothing, slobber on our shirts, mess up our hair, and go down to the Walmart photo studio and redo the same photo as adults. We all laughed off the idea until we began to talk through what we would have to do to pull it off. The more we talked about it, the funnier it became. Our imaginations were stirred and we got so happy and excited that we decided we had to go through with it. So we all got messed up until we looked pretty close to our childhood photo, and off we went to Walmart. When we arrived, the lady at the counter looked at us, and then looked again. She asked if she could help us. We said that we wanted to take a family photo. She asked if we were sure. We answered yes as we laughed at her shocked expression. "Don't you want to get cleaned up first?" she countered. We laughed hysterically as we pulled out our childhood photo to show her, and I explained my bright idea.

Her expression became less confused the more we filled in the blanks for her. Then she commented, "Well, I think that is the cutest thing in the world." After that, she was in the moment with us and she happily went ahead with our photo shoot. We left afterwards with silly smiles on our faces that lasted the rest of the day.

There was something about that silly act that drew us back to our childhood memories and the closeness we shared when we were kids. We were remembering and cherishing each other. Being together again in that way brought us great joy. That week is still talked about as one of the greatest experiences in our family. Coming together as a family was extremely revitalizing for all of us.

God's family is very big. According to the book of Ephesians, the family is separated into two places, Heaven and Earth. He calls it the *whole family*. A whole family is not complete without all of its members.

Some family members are in Heaven . . .

In 2010, I was riding in a van in Nigeria with the members of our team. We had stayed with Mummy Audu, the widow of a former Nigerian ambassador to the United Nations. She and her daughter Ross were our hosts for a few days as we rested from a grueling ministry schedule, which required many hours on the road. They took great care of us.

Her husband, a very ambitious medical doctor, had worked tirelessly helping his people. He had built a hospital, built schools, pastored a church for 25 years, and became the ambassador from Nigeria to the United Nations. Many people had come to know them as Mummy and Daddy.

Their family extended past flesh and blood to include the city they lived in; a community of churches and ministries, and ultimately the entire Nation of Nigeria; an ever expanding family. This family is not only well known in Nigeria, but also in Heaven. Daddy is already there. And many of the people he served while on the Earth are in Heaven. At one point in the future, all of us will become a part of the family that is in Heaven, because we all have an appointed time. Of course, many of the Nigerian saints who paved the way for Daddy were in Heaven centuries before Daddy. Everyone in Heaven has a history here on Earth.

While riding from northern Nigeria to the south, our trip was 17 hours. Part of the way through, we crossed a bridge that spanned the Niger River. As we crossed, there was a town built there. Small wooden boats were at the shore. Fishermen were mending their nets. The boats were all hand-made as were the nets. It put me in mind of what it must have been like when Jesus called the sons of Zebedee, James and his brother John to follow him with the promise of making them fishers of men.

Macphilips Jasper, my beloved bishop and evangelist, told me that the city was an ancient city. When he said this, the Lord Jesus revealed something about the whole family in Heaven and in Earth.

He shared with me that right now there are multitudes of saints in Heaven who used to live in that city. Through the ages, they called out to God and many of them had prayed about the days that I live in. They had a family, just like me. They loved their family just like I love mine. They had prayed for their future descendants and had believed God to look out for them, to save them, to prosper them, and so on.

These saints were born there, married there, raised their children there, and were buried there. They prayed to God about their descendants, looking through time just like the prophets of old who saw into our day and rejoiced. He said those in Heaven had prayed into the day that I live in. They had prayed for the city and the people who were living there right now. He then said that there is no expiration date on their prayers. The people in Heaven are counting on us to complete them. They want us to be the answer to the prayers they prayed all those years ago. We have a mission to do the work of the Lord in our generation.

I realized for the first time that what I do for the Lord is because someone in Heaven has prayed for it to happen. When I thought about this, I realized that when I come to Heaven, there will be a multitude of Nigerians that would greet me and thank me for laboring in their nation and being God's answer to at least some of their prayers. What an honor it is to imagine that I can be such a blessing. It really changed how I saw things.

One day, there is going to be a family reunion. The whole family will be together. We will all be without pain and sorrow; perfectly whole and wonderfully connected. I can't wait for that day. And on that day, we will be reunited with many we have known on the Earth. What an interesting thought.

> And these all, having obtained a good report through faith, received not the promise: God having provided some better thing for us, that they without us should not be made perfect. (Hebrews 11:39–40)

We are not whole without the members of our family in Heaven, and without us, they are imperfect.

What we do on the Earth with what we have been given in Christ brings perfection for those who came before us. They have an interest in what we do here on Earth. They are very interested in us; they believe for us that we will become aware of our purpose and fulfill the destiny we have. The choices we make here have an impact on them.

Just as the Ambassador's family kept on expanding the Kingdom of God, bringing more and more family members into the sheepfold, I too have the same mission, and so do you. What we do matters forever. There is an eternal purpose to what we do here. The whole family in Heaven and in Earth benefit for eternity when we live out God's purpose.

> Wherefore seeing we also are compassed about with so great a cloud of witnesses, let us lay aside every weight, and the sin which doth so easily beset us, and let us run with patience the race that is set before us. (Hebrews 12:1)

Our family in Heaven is called the *cloud of witnesses*. My grandmothers have been there for a long time already. The Bible names some of our family members, but others are mentioned by what they accomplished and by what they endured.

> Who through faith subdued kingdoms, wrought righteousness, obtained promises, stopped the mouths of lions, quenched the violence of fire, escaped the edge of the sword, out of weakness were made strong, waxed valiant in fight, turned to flight the armies of the aliens. Women received their dead raised to life again: and others were tortured, not accepting deliverance; that they might obtain a better resurrection: And others had trial of cruel mockings and scourgings, yea, moreover of bonds and imprisonment: They were stoned, they were sawn asunder, were tempted, were slain with the sword: they wandered about in sheepskins and goatskins; being destitute, afflicted, tormented. (Hebrews 11:33–37)

These same atrocities are carried out all over the world every day. Every day, Christians are slaughtered somewhere in the world because of their faith in Christ.

FAMILY TREES

A rapidly growing trend is family tree searches. Online companies provide great tools to find family records. In less than three months, my sister Laurie went back hundreds of years. As it turns out, there were notable ancestors in our family tree. A great-great-grandfather signed the constitution of the original California Republic; another grandfather was a revolutionary war hero.

Remembering them inspires me and reconnects me to them. I have yet to meet them, but they are a part of me and I of them. We are flesh and blood. We carry the same DNA.

I can't wait to meet them. I want to find out what they asked God for. How they lived. What traits do I have that were passed down. This excites me. God is not the God of the dead, but of the living. My ancestors are alive. They have become part of the cloud of witnesses.

My friend Gary Hicks and I went to Edmonton, Alberta, Canada to pass out gospel tracts on a summer day. Before hitting the streets, we stopped at a friend's house to meet up for prayer before going. She had a couple of friends with her, Linda and her daughter Alanna, who would also join us that day.

As we got to know them, we learned that Linda's husband died six months earlier from a lifetime illness. He had been very courageous and was well respected by many. His passing hit them very hard. Like many who have lost a loved one, they spoke of him in the past tense: "He was" and "He used to be." In fact, they didn't speak his name at all for quite some time.

On the way to our destination, I rode with these ladies sitting in the back seat alone as they occupied the front seats. We kept talking about their lost family member. They kept using past-tense language when referring to him. As I listened, the Lord was moving upon me, so instead of asking what the husband's, name **was**; I asked them what his name **is.** When I said *is*, they became quiet for a moment and finally said his name **is** Ron.

I asked them what Ron **is** like. Again, *is* refers more to *one living* than one *who used to live*. I think they enjoyed my questions, so they talked about Ron, remembering how wonderful their time with him was, sharing his qualities and inspiring courage and fearlessness in the face of adversity. I kept thinking what a wonderful brother Ron **is.** I started to minister to them while we drove. I began with a story.

"My Grandmother Estephana Hanks is a very spiritual person. She was a catholic believer, in whom I first saw the power of God. My siblings and I lived with Grandma for a time after my parents were divorced. She had 13 kids, all of which were older than my Dad except for the twins. Rudy and Raymond were the babies and they intermittently lived at Grandma's house. They were alcoholics and got in the occasional fight; sometimes they would get into a fist fight, knocking over furniture and rolling around on the floor. One day Rudy was very angry and was complaining and yelling. It was very tense. My Grandma grabbed a crucifix off the wall, came up behind Rudy, and held the crucifix behind his head without him knowing she was there. Instantly, his rage came to a complete stop and he was peaceful. It happened so fast that it got my attention. There was something about Estephana that was supernatural.

She was getting much older then and sat for long periods of time in an old comfortable chair. Her time was divided into three activities, praying with her rosary, sleeping, and crocheting. She did this day in and day out."

I told these ladies that if it were not for my Grandmother, I don't know if I would be serving God today. Grandma prayed for us, she believed God had a plan for us. I believe it was because of her prayers that her family kept on going.

"Grandma has joined what the Bible calls *so great a cloud of witnesses.* She is in Heaven right now observing us. She is listening to our conversation right now. Do you know who is standing beside her right now? Ron is. He is alive—they are both alive because God is not the God of the dead but of the living. They are witnessing what we are doing, everything we are saying, and they have a keen interest in our lives."

It was about this time that it seemed as though the cloud of witnesses had entered into the car with us as we drove. Heaven had come to attention. Truth was being shared that God really wanted Linda and Alanna to understand. They began to cry as I continued.

"Ron and Grandma are smiling now; they have an understanding that we have yet to know. They are in Heaven and know many things about us that Jesus has already shown them. Do you know what Ron is saying right now? He is saying "I love you both very much. Jesus has already shown me that you will be fine; He is taking care of you, and you must look forward. You can do it, you will keep going. God is with you." These exhortations did not come from me, but seemed to flow through me. They went on for a few minutes longer. The passion and love in the voice and the presence of Heaven in the car caused us all to weep in a glorious atmosphere of divine healing love. It was indescribable.

We got quiet for a while as we drove the rest of the way downtown. When we got out of the car, we gathered ourselves and began to walk together to the place we would join up with Gary and my friend Pam. As we walked, I asked Linda: "was it just me, or did Heaven come into the car with us?"

Linda said "Oh Frank, when you told us what Ron was saying, you sounded exactly like him, you talked to Alanna just like he spoke with her, using his tone and expressions in a way that was strictly between them. If you had used her nickname that Ron used to call her by, I would have wrecked the car. That's how real it was!"

Our encounter was heavenly. There we were, right in the middle of the cloud of witnesses while driving in a car. There was so much power in that car that anything could have happened. But most important to Linda and Alanna was that God touched them in the deepest part of their grief. I have never encountered such a visitation before.

I now refer to it as ministering in the cloud; our Family in Heaven, partnering with our family on Earth. I never knew such manifestations existed. I was simply following a trail of breadcrumbs that the Holy Spirit was guiding me by. There was great power in re-membering our whole family.

Something else happened in the car that day that I realized after we talked later. I told Linda that although I had never met her husband Ron, I feel I know him and I love him very much. I asked her if that made any sense. She said that it did, because after hearing of my Grandma, she felt she knew her and loved her as well.

I don't know how that works, except to say that through Christ we are eternally connected. Heaven's reality is that you know and love even those family members whom you've never met on Earth. The atmosphere of Heaven permeated us, leaving its indelible qualities etched in our earthly realm within our hearts. Pervasive love is part of the inheritance of the Saints in light. I want more of it. It comes from my heavenly home where everyone is family and all are completely loved by one another. It's Heaven invading the Earth.

> The secret things belong unto the Lord our God: but those things which are revealed belong unto us and to our children forever, that we may do all the words of this law. (Deuteronomy 29:29)

This revelation of the cloud of witnesses was hidden from us before our car ride to do street ministry. But, it supernaturally unfolded as we began playing in a supernatural sand box like children, discovering the mystery and the reality of the cloud of witnesses. Their love for us is far beyond our current understanding. They reside in a perfect atmosphere of holy love. All the pain of this world is past them, but a deeper understanding of who we are and the trials that we face are very familiar to them.

- They understand the difficulties of raising your hands to praise God when your life feels like combat.

- They understand what it feels like when your baby has died, or your children make painful choices.

- They know what it is like to suffer persecution and to be rejected or shamefully abused.

- They know what it is like to be tortured and killed because of a faith in Jesus Christ.

Their Love for us; their family still on Earth, is powerful. They are whole, fully alive in the love of God and lacking nothing. But, they will not be satisfied until what is true in this holy atmosphere, is also true on Earth: thy kingdom come, thy will be done on Earth as it is in Heaven.

There is untapped power in being connected to your family in Heaven and on Earth.

Looking unto Jesus the author and finisher of our faith; who for the joy that was set before him endured the cross, despising the shame, and is set down at the right hand of the throne of God. For consider him that endured such contradiction of sinners against himself, lest ye be wearied and faint in your minds. Ye have not yet resisted unto blood, striving against sin. (Hebrews 12:2-4)

Reaching into your heavenly family tree for inspiration is something the writer of the book of Hebrews encourages us to do. This great cloud of family members who finished well and gave witness to Jesus and to His resurrection; they are real. When we honor them and their memories, we are strengthened and inspired to continue to follow Jesus. We are remembering them. Their prayers throughout every age are stored up, along with every resource in Heaven that is required to make us whole. Perhaps the word *whole* has a dual meaning:

complete as a family, and wholeness in Christ. We are all complete in Him.

Just as Jesus is the author and finisher of their faith, He is yours as well. Look to him. He has a plan for the whole family in Heaven and on Earth. The family in Heaven has an interest in the events of our lives here. We are all the body of Christ, both here and there. They have seen our day and rejoice in the undefeatable plan of the Author.

Jump back into His plan with your whole heart. Set your affections on things above and not on the Earth beneath. The game plan is glorious when you see it from Heaven's vantage point. Let's rule and reign with Him in this life through the free gift of righteousness and join a great company of those who have already finished well and wear a crown of Gold. Praise the Lord!

9

STORIES

God has people who are and have been doing the impossible in the earth. They have taken Jesus at his word and have stepped up to become the miracle workers of their generation. Outstanding and mind-blowing miracles have been the result. Body parts appearing out of nowhere, sight available from an eye socket without an eyeball and an arm missing from below the shoulder growing out before the eyes of a great crowd. These are but a few of these miracles but many more will follow as we take our place doing miracles in our generation. Enjoy these stories

REVEREND LUELLA YOUNGMAN
Man Receives New Arm

In Ghana in 1953, at an outdoor meeting, two women were praying for the sick. A man suffering from leprosy approached Reverend Luella Youngman for prayer. Not only does leprosy eat away flesh, but also bone. When Luella first saw this man, she didn't notice that the man was missing his right arm from midway between the elbow and shoulder; leprosy had taken the better part of his arm.

As Luella reached out to pray for the man, she was shocked to see that his arm was growing out before her eyes, before she touched him. She watched as his arm grew a new elbow, forearm and finally a beautiful hand that was a perfect match to his other one.

Reverend Luella claims the atmosphere was one where the power of God was present to heal, and that His power was healing leprosy and every other infirmity amongst the people. Her astonishment at this new body part growing out before her eyes was so strong, she still cannot remember the look on the man's face or anything else about that moment. But, whenever she recalls this creative miracle, she can see it clearly in her spirit, and the very same awe that she felt in that moment comes back to her as though she were still standing there. A deep appreciation for the love of God and how wonderful He is cannot help to surface as this elder saint and missionary tells of this miracle.

Luella claims that if Jesus is Lord, than the only right response to Him is obedience.

> He that hath my commandments, and keepeth them, he it is that loveth me: and he that loveth me shall be loved of my Father, and I will love him, and will manifest myself to him. (John 14:21)

Luella steps out in faith when she brings someone noticeably crippled, blind or otherwise to the front of a crowd so that people can witness them being healed. The people go wild because they have never witnessed a miracle before. Once she performs the first miracle, it's pretty much a party after that. Miracles begin to break out everywhere in the crowd. To me, this speaks of the willingness of Jesus to break out all over the place once someone gives Him access by opening the way to Him, the one who is the same yesterday, today and forever.

One day, Luella shared a key with me that I will never forget.

"Jesus has shown me that there is a key to every altar call. When I call people forth for healing, I simply wait for God to show me which person is ready to receive a miracle. It may take a few minutes, but I just pray in tongues silently and He always shows me. I then go to the person and pray for them. Every time they are healed instantly, and then the faith of everyone rises as miracles break out one after the other."

I am honored to know Luella because she has served the Lord on the mission fields in Canada's north for over 50 years. She and her husband Alex, who has already gone to be with the Lord, wore out two airplanes, travelled by boat and dog sled, and had many brushes with death. They had fellowship with many great men of God, such as Lester Summeral, Jack Coe and others. I like to pray with Luella and I love hearing her share her testimonies of Jesus Christ. I am grateful that God has allowed me the privilege of knowing this mighty woman of God and for allowing me to call her my friend.

RONALD COYNE

Able to See from an Empty Eye Socket

In 1951, in Sapulpa, Oklahoma, seven-year-old Ronald Coyne had his right eyeball surgically removed after an accident. Ten months later, during a Miracle Tent Crusade, Ronald suddenly began to see through his empty eye socket as a result of the lady evangelist prayer.

This miracle shocked the world as young Ronald was tested by many doctors who verified that although Ronald had no eye ball in his eye socket he was still able to see. Many reporters wanted to interview Ronald and some were allowed to. Ronald travelled the world giving Glory to God and demonstrating his ability to see. He was on many TV shows were he testified of His miracle and about the Love of God.

BOB LOVELACE

New Disc
Red Deer, Alberta

Bob had a disc in his back that was totally flat; his vertebrae were rubbing together causing lots of pain. Although Bob had operations to fuse the discs together, the pain persisted for years. One morning while a visiting minister was ministering healing to those in church, he invited anyone who needed healing to come forward for prayer. Bob stayed in his seat, too shy to come forward. Afterwards, he regretted not going forward, fearing he had missed his chance to be healed.

That night, Bob returned to church for the evening service. The pastor was teaching on healing as the visiting minister was no longer there. Bob listened intently to the teaching all the while wishing he had responded earlier in the day. But as he was listening, the pastor made a statement Bob will never forget. He said, "When you are being healed, you will feel heat in the area of your infirmity; this is a sign that God is healing you." When Bob heard that statement, he felt a soothing heat flow from the top of his head right down his back. This happened three times during the remainder of the service. His pain was still there, but over the next 21 days, this heat would show up in the same way. At the end of this time, Bob had a brand-new disc, replacing the damaged one. He has the cat scan of the collapsed discs and an x-ray showing the new body part. Praise The Lord!

STAN HERON
New Lungs
Red Deer, Alberta

Stan Heron suffered from *chronic obstructive pulmonary disease* (COPD), which is a lung condition that limited Stan to very shallow breathing. His attempts to take large breaths would cause painful choking coughs and pain in his lungs. Stan's mobility and energy levels were greatly affected for several years.

I had been fellowshipping with Stan's brother Russ and his wife Debi. After a few meetings together, I gave him a chapter from my two books, *Body Parts* and *Training Wheels*. After reading, he came alive with the revelation that anyone can perform miracles and he wanted to perform them.

Russ called me and wanted to meet. We met for half hour when Russ's brother Stan came in and sat down with Russ, Debi and I. We spoke for a while. Stan had recently received Jesus and was newly baptized. After talking with Stan for some time and imparting some spiritual gifts to him, Russ said, "Stan suffers from COPD. I believe God has a brand-new pair of lungs ready to put in Stan's chest." I asked Russ what he saw. He said he saw two perfect lungs, pink and healthy, just waiting for Stan." So, I asked Russ what he intended to do about it and whether he was willing to pray for him. He said yes, reached across the table, laid his hands on his brother's chest, and commanded a brand-new set of lungs be put into his brother's chest in the name of Jesus.

Almost immediately, Stan began taking deep breaths; a few days later he reported overall improvements in health and circulation, and new vitality. Stan is doing many things now that he has not been able to do for years. There was something about Stan. When I met him, he had a real faith In Jesus and in God's ability to do anything. It was exciting to be around him. Praise the Lord.

PASTOR DOUG KLAN

Healing CD
Raising a Man from the Dead

Recently, I had the pleasure of meeting with Pastor Doug Klan from the Word of Faith church in Edmonton, who performs a steady stream of miracles. His wife tells him how she notices he is in his happiest place when he is praying for the sick and performing miracles. I witnessed his joy as well, as he lit up when sharing with me how Jesus has walked with him for many years and as he told of some of the miracles he's witnessed. Another notable quality was Doug's desire to enable and empower others to walk in faith.

Of particular interest to me was how God told him to make a tape of healing Scriptures to give out or to sell in their book store. He wondered why he should make a tape when so many have already done so, like Kenneth Copeland and Kenneth Hagin ministries. But God told him again, and finally he did.

Before he packaged it, he had a copy sitting on his desk. While ministering to a woman one day, God told him to give her a copy of the CD with the following instructions: "Tell her to listen to it all night long with the volume just high enough not to wake her up." This woman followed his instructions and was healed. This has happened many times over when people were diligent to use the CD.

Doug also shared this testimony of the first man he raised from the dead. He wrote these words:

> I was asked to tell you about a young boy that was raised from the dead. I was preaching in Rankin Inlet and was holding meeting in an arena hall. The third day, I was teaching and this young man on the second row fell to the floor. As he went down, he knocked some chairs around. I thought he had just fallen asleep and was waiting for him to get back up in his chair. Some people went over to see what happened. One of them was a nurse. She tried to find his pulse and yelled, "Someone call 911; his heart is not beating."
>
> I had an anger rise up in me and I thought no one is dying in my meetings. I walked over to him and command the spirit of death to go, and I commanded him to come back to life in the name of Jesus. Immediately he sat up and asked what happened. He got up and sat down completely normal. I continued to teach. The ambulance showed up and examined him and could not find anything wrong with him. His heart was beating normally and all his vitals were normal. The word went out in Rankin Inlet and people came out to hear the word had greatly increased. Thanks for allowing me to share.

The stories here are but a sampling of the many creative miracles which happen around the world on a regular basis. Saints the world over are beginning to ask the Lord for these uncommon manifestations. After all why are we not asking for brand-new organs; a brand-new part would be superior to a used one. I believe the time has come for us to step into the calling to perform miracles just as Jesus did when he was on the earth elevate your imagination and appropriate the prophetic strands of divine DNA. You are capable of far more than you have imagined. May the Lord pour out his spirit upon all flesh, saints and sinners alike.

THE END

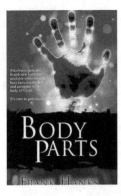

Other titles from Frank Hanks include:

TRAINING WHEELS

HOW TO GET KICKED OUT OF CHURCH

The Author is open to publishers wishing to translate and or acquire distribution rights internationally. Agents welcome

Order any of Frank's books by the case for Bible studies:

- 25 books per case
- More than 10 cases = $8.00 per book + shipping and handling
- Prices for books going to missions organizations are favorably negotiable at any quantity

Order books direct from: Empty Hospitals Publishing:

E-mail: emptyhospitals@gmail.com.

Website: www.emptyhospitals.org

Mailing Address:
Empty Hospitals Publishing
PO Box 28013 Highland Green
Red Deer, AB. T4N 7C2

Ministry Information:

Contact Frank Hanks and his ministry about speaking in mass harvest campaigns, conferences, revival meetings or to receive more information about his ministry:

E-mail: emptyhospitals@gmail.com.
Website: www.emptyhospitals.org

Mailing Address:
Empty Hospitals International
PO Box 28013 Highland Green
Red Deer, AB. T4N 7C2

CPSIA information can be obtained
at www.ICGtesting.com
Printed in the USA
BVHW041128200621
609990BV00025B/774